DO GEESE GET GOOSE BUMPS?

& more than 199 perplexing questions with astounding answers

"I HAVE NO SPECIAL TALENTS. I AM ONLY PASSIONATELY CURIOUS."

—ALBERT EINSTEIN

Portable Press/The Bathroom Readers' Institute
An imprint of Printers Row Publishing Group
10350 Barnes Canyon Road, Suite 100, San Diego, CA 92121
www.portablepress.com
e-mail: mail@bathroomreader.com

Printers Row Publishing Group is a division of Readerlink Distribution
Services, LLC.

The Portable Press name and logo are trademarks of Readerlink
Distribution Services, LLC.

All correspondence concerning the content of this book should be
addressed to Portable Press/The Bathroom Readers' Institute,
Editorial Department, at the above address.

Library of Congress Cataloging-in-Publication Data
Names: Portable Press (San Diego, Ca.)
Title: Do geese get goose bumps? / the Bathroom Readers' Institute.
Description: San Diego, Ca : Portable Press, 2016.
Identifiers: LCCN 2016003537 | ISBN 9781626867543 (hardcover)
Subjects: LCSH: Curiosities and wonders. | BISAC: REFERENCE /
Trivia.
Classification: LCC AG244 .D53 2016 | DDC 031.02--dc23

Printed in the United States of America

First Printing
20 19 18 17 16   1 2 3 4 5

THANK YOU

Gordon Javna

Jay Newman

Megan Todd

Brandon Hartley

Trina Janssen

Andy Taray

Dan Mansfield

Derek Fairbridge

Brian Boone

John Dollison

Thom Little

Kim Griswell

Aaron Guzman

Melinda Allman

Peter Norton

Lilian Nordland

Curious George

TABLE OF CONTENTS

INTRODUCTION

"Why?"

There is no question more succinct—and more wide-reaching—than that one. The first time that our toddler brains thought to ask "why?" was when our worlds really started taking shape, growing us into the curious creatures we are.

"Why is the sky blue?" "Why does the dog wag his tail?" "Why do I have to go to sleep?" may seem like kid stuff, but they're fascinating questions with fascinating answers...and that's what you'll find in this book.

So if you, like us, have an insatiable curiosity to learn more about, well, everything—history, science, technology, language, nature, pop culture, and a whole lot more—you've come to the right place. In *Do Geese Get Goose Bumps?*, you'll find out why basketballs are orange, why decaf coffee pots are orange, and which came first: the color orange or the name of the fruit. You'll learn why ghosts wear white sheets, why Abraham Lincoln wore a tall top hat, and, of course, you'll find out whether geese get goose bumps.

So sit back and settle in for a knowlegde dump unlike anything you've ever experienced...since you were three.

AROUND
THE HOUSE

TANGLED UP AND BLUE

Q: How do cords get tangled?

A: You pull off your ear buds and absentmindedly toss
them into your pocket. The next time you reach for
them, the cord has somehow become tangled, knotted,
and bunched up several times over. How could this
happen? There wasn't even anything else in there! This
mysterious affliction also affects extension cords,
Christmas lights, curtain strings, and more. The culprits: cord gremlins. These nasty little beasties sneak in
when you're not around and laugh maniacally as they
mangle your cord into a tangled headache.

And if you don't buy that explanation, there's
actually a scientific discipline devoted solely to understanding this exact conundrum. It's called "knot
theory." Proponents of this (admittedly small) discipline
have used complex mathematic formulas to prove that
there is almost a 100 percent chance that something
that *can* knot in storage *will* knot in storage. That's
because, even though there is only one way for a cord
to be untangled, there are hundreds of ways for it to
get tangled in the first place. There are countless types
and styles of knots, and they can combine with each
other in any way you can imagine—and in some ways
you can't.

Any place on the cord at which it can bend is called
a *contact point*. The more contact points on a cord, the
more possibilities there are for the cord to bend and
thus knot itself. Pliable cords for headphones and

Christmas lights have so many contact points that tiny changes in the environment—even temperature varia- tions—can cause those contact points to bend, move, and wrap around each other. Let's say those ear buds are in your coat pocket and you placed the coat gently over a chair. That little bit of motion is enough to make the cord bend in at least one place, but probably more. Then you pick up the coat (more bending), put it on (more bending), and start walking toward the door (more bending). By the time you get to get the ear buds out of your pocket, the cord is all knotted up.

The only way to keep this from happening: properly wrap or store your cord in such a way that it can't tangle. When it comes to headphone cords, wrapping them around a small piece of cardboard should keep them safe from the cord gremlins.

BREAKING DOWN

Q: How does soap work?

A: Just combine it with warm or hot water, and soap always seems to know just how to get rid of the grime you don't want on your skin (or your clothes, dishes, bathroom sink, etc.), and not remove anything else but the grime. The underlying scientific principle is quite simple, and it's a variant of the old adage "oil and water don't mix." It's true: oil and water really don't mix, so when you wash your hands with soap and water, the soap breaks down the impurities on your hands (which consist partially of naturally occurring oils, along with other stuff) into smaller molecules. Soap is made from ingredients that are *hydrophilic* at one end and *hydrophobic* at the other, which means they are attracted to and repel water, respectively.

As the tap water—along with the water present in the soap itself—breaks down dirt and oils into smaller molecules, the hydrophobic molecules in the soap attach themselves to those increasingly smaller dirt and oil bits. This creates a new kind of oil droplet, one that's smaller than a water molecule. And because of the hydrophilic soap molecules, this droplet is attracted to that water. The dirt becomes absorbed inside of the water molecule…which washes right off your hands and then goes down the drain.

COUNTER CULTURE

Q: Why do coffee stains leave a ring?

A: If you've never noticed it before, you will the next time you see a dried coffee stain on a table or a counter—the outside of the stain has become a dark brown border, while the inside of the stain is almost completely gone. What's going on? It's actually quite fascinating.

When the coffee, which is made up of water and coffee grounds, spills onto a flat surface, it starts spreading out in every direction. The flow stops when it hits something, usually a tiny crack or crevice that you can't even see. That's why spilled coffee is shaped like a haphazard splotch instead of a perfect circle (because truly flat surfaces are very rare).

Once the coffee stain settles, the water starts evaporating. That occurs on the outer edges first, because the puddle is the thinnest there. Along with evaporation comes replenishment. The coffee is pulled from the center out to the edges to replenish the evaporated bits, and the tiny coffee grounds are pulled all the way to the edges of the splotch and then collect in the tiny crevices that shaped the stain. After the water is gone, all that's left of the spill has collected along the dark brown edges.

ONE CLUMP OR TWO?

Q: How does clumping kitty litter work?

A: Modern cat litter has been around since the late 1940s. It was invented by Ed Lowe, who worked at an industrial absorbents company in Michigan, after his neighbor complained that her cat tracked the ash she was using in a box all over the house. Looking for a better solution, Lowe used an absorbent clay called Fuller's Earth, which he called "kitty litter," and later marketed as Tidy Cat.

But it didn't clump.

That technology was developed a few decades later by adding a chemical to Fuller's Earth called *bentonite*, which holds the clay together when it gets wet. How? It contains absorbent sodium ions that have a high hydration sphere, which attracts water molecules. That's the process that makes the urine clump together in a sphere.

Bonus Fact: Some experts warn that clumping litter can be unhealthy for cats that lick themselves after going to the box. Some of the litter can clump inside their intestines, potentially causing blockages. It can also lead to constipation, diarrhea, and urinary tract infections. However, there are no scientific studies that prove clumping litters are harmful, and if you do try to switch to a non-clay litter (usually made of wheat), don't be surprised if your cat refuses to use it.

SOME QUESTIONS HAVE NO ANSWERS

"At the ballet, you see girls dancing on their tiptoes. Why don't they just get taller girls?"

—GREG RAY

PILLS BURY

Q: Why is there cotton in my medicine?

A: There's a ball of cotton in every factory-sealed pill bottle so consumers will subconsciously think of cotton candy. It makes the medicine go down easier.

Just kidding.

The primary reason for the cotton ball is to keep the pills, capsules, or tablets from rattling around in the bottle and breaking or leaking. But that's not all: the cotton also reduces the ambient moisture that could potentially upset the medicine's chemical balance and affect its potency. And it's not really cotton—at least not entirely. The pharmaceutical industry calls the stuff "filler," and it's made of a combination of cotton, rayon, and polyester.

TOO MUCH OF A GOOD THING

Q: Why is it so dangerous to take certain medications with grapefruit juice?

A: Grapefruit juice can interfere with cholesterol-lowering medications, heart pills, allergy pills, antidepressants, and dozens of other medicines. But wait, isn't grapefruit—which is chock-full of vitamin C—supposed to be one of the healthier fruits? Yes, but it is as just as chemically complex as those medications.

Grapefruit juice is rife with chemical compounds called *furanocoumarins*. Otherwise harmless to humans, they're a naturally occurring defense mechanism that help grapefruit (and many other plants) ward off insects, bacteria, and even some mammals. Furanocoumarins are found in lots of foods, particularly citrus fruits, but they're found in the highest quantities in grapefruit juice.

If you're taking certain medicines and then drink a glass of grapefruit juice, the furanocoumarins can interfere with your body's process of breaking down the drugs and sending the medicine where it needs to go.

This doesn't mean it prevents the medicine from being effective. Quite the opposite. Instead, the body doesn't break down the medication and accepts it whole, which results in an extremely high dosage.

This could potentially cause a lot of damage. For example, heart medications that are delivered in too high of a dose could lead to blood clots or arrhythmia. Too much of a statin could lower blood cholesterol levels way too far. So if you're on one of these medications and want to drink some fruit juice, try grape juice instead—but doctors recommend that you drink a lot of water.

THE PITS

Q: What's the difference between an underarm deodorant and an antiperspirant?

A: To answer that question, we first must ask why armpits smell so bad in the first place. The answer: bacteria poop. The sweat that you perspire is mostly odorless. But the sweat that emits from your apocrine glands (in your underarms) is full of organic-rich proteins. After a while, the bacteria that live on your skin start eating those proteins; when they break them down, the waste products cause the nasty odor.

So if you're wondering whether to buy an antiperspirant or a deodorant, know that both products are designed to kill bacteria. But that's all a deodorant does. An antiperspirant has another ingredient—aluminum—that obstructs the flow of perspiration as well.

And it doesn't take a whole lot of a roll-on antiperspi-rant to do the job—just one roll of the roll-on (when your underarms are a bit moist, experts say) should coat the follicles enough to block the sweat and starve the bacteria.

HOT STUFF

Q: **Why does a pile of grass clippings get hot in the middle?**

A: Rotting grass is the result of some complex chemical changes, one of the by-products of which is heat. And because the rotting begins deep inside the pile, it gets hot inside there.

TO B OR NOT TO B

Q: **There are A, C, and D batteries, but no B batteries. Why?**

A: Stand-up comedian Demetri Martin came up with a possible reason for the lack of B batteries: "I think it's to avoid confusion. Because if there were B batteries, you wouldn't know when someone was stuttering." (Rim shot.) Well, Demetri, there actually are B batteries, but they're not sold in the United States because there aren't many products that require that particular size of battery (which is what the letters refer to—size—the higher the letter, the bigger the battery). So what are B batteries mostly used for? Bicycle lamps in Europe.

There are A batteries as well, and E and F sizes, too. But because they aren't used in most consumer products, retail stores don't sell them. (Old ham radio enthusiasts are familiar with A and B batteries, but those were used for vacuum tubes and not for consumer products.)

A NO-WIN SCENARIO

Q: Paper or plastic?

A: If possible, choose neither—that's if you're even given the choice at your local supermarket. Let's look at the pros and cons of both.

Plastic grocery bags certainly get the worst press; they've been outlawed in many areas and are being phased out in others. Since they were introduced in 1977, trillions of plastic bags have found their way into lakes and oceans, where they can harm wildlife that mistake them for food. Plus, they're made from ethylene, a by-product of oil, gas, and coal production—all nonrenewable resources. The petroleum used to make 14 plastic bags is enough to drive a typical car one mile. What's more, plastic bags may take up to 1,000 years to decompose.

But paper bags aren't much better. For one, they come from trees. Although wood is a renewable resource, it's a slow-growing one: It takes a tree several years to grow from a seedling to harvestable size. And manufacturing one paper bag creates 70 percent more air pollutants and 50 times more water pollutants than making a plastic bag; that's not to mention the gallon of water needed to produce every single one. And because paper bags are larger and heavier than plastic ones, fewer can be transported per truck, which results in higher fuel consumption.

Plastic bags require less energy, oil, and water to produce compared with a paper bag made with 30 percent recycled content, but they take a long time to break down. Paper bags break down in a fraction of the time. According to the U.S. Environmental Protection Agency, it takes 91 percent more energy to recycle a pound of paper than it does to recycle a pound of plastic.

The best solution: buy some sturdy cloth bags and use them over and over.

WHAT THE BRICK?!

Q: **Why does it hurt so much when you step on a Lego?**

A: For most of human history, we didn't have shoes, so in order to traverse an unforgiving landscape without getting injured, the bottoms of our feet developed extra pain sensors. The more a body part hurts, the quicker the nervous system will react to removing it from the pain source. And the pain caused by Legos—with their hard, sharp corners—mimics the dangerous ground objects—quills, sharp rocks, etc.—that could take a hunter-gatherer out of the game. In fact, the bottom of your feet have more pain receptors per square inch than almost anywhere else on your body.

You have two main types of pain receptors: *C fibers*, which detect slow, lingering pain, and *A-delta fibers*, which detect more acute pain. There are more than 200,000 A-delta receptors in the bottoms of your feet, more per square inch than anywhere else on your body.

Another factor at play is the chemical makeup of the Legos themselves. According to the American Chemical Society, the bricks are made of ABS plastic—a terpolymer, which has three main monomers: one for strength, one for resistance, and one for shininess. Combined, they make the little bricks very strong. And in order for Legos to fit together so snugly, the edges must be formed at exact right angles, which makes them quite sharp.

When you step on an errant Lego at 3:00 a.m. on your way to the bathroom, the full force of your weight impacts on the Lego. The brick's strength doesn't give at all, causing the sharp edges to protrude far into your skin—impacting all of those A-delta receptors—which transmit pain signals to your brain faster than you can yell, "Who left that $@#% Lego on the floor?!"

SOME QUESTIONS HAVE NO ANSWERS

"Why are women so much more interesting to men than men are to women?"

—VIRGINIA WOOLF

THE MAGIC BOX

Q: How does a microwave oven work?

A: To answer that, we need to know what microwaves are. Put simply, they are waves of electromagnetic energy, just like visible light, radio waves, and X-rays. What makes these four waves differ from each other? Each has a different length (wavelength) and vibrates at a different speed (frequency). Microwaves get their name because their wavelength is much shorter than electromagnetic waves that carry TV and radio signals.

The microwaves in a microwave oven have a wavelength of about four inches, and they vibrate 2.5 billion times per second—about the same natural frequency as water molecules. That's what makes them so effective at heating food. A conventional oven heats the air in the oven, which then cooks the food. But microwaves cause water molecules inside the food itself to vibrate at high speeds, creating heat. The heated water molecules are what cook the food. Glass, ceramic, and paper plates contain virtually no water molecules, which is why they don't get too hot in the microwave.

Here's how it works: when you press the start button, electricity passes through the *magnetron*, the tube that produces microwaves. The microwaves are then channeled down a metal tube (waveguide) and through a slowly rotating metal fan (stirrer), which scatters them into the part of the oven where the food is placed. The walls of the oven are made of metal, which reflects microwaves the same way that a mirror reflects visible light. So when the microwaves hit the stirrer and are scattered into the food chamber, they bounce off the metal walls and penetrate the food from every direction. Most ovens have a rotating turntable that helps food cook more evenly.

HOME-COOKED SHMEAL

Q: Why doesn't food cooked in a microwave taste as good as food cooked in the oven?

A: According to legend, shortly after Raytheon perfected its first microwave oven in the 1950s, Charles Adams, the chairman of Raytheon, had one installed in his kitchen so he could taste for himself what micro-wave-cooked food was like. But as Adams's cook quickly discovered, meat didn't brown in the oven, french fries stayed limp and damp, and cakes didn't rise. The cook, condemning the oven as "black magic," quit.

When sales of microwave ovens took off in the late 1980s, millions of cooks discovered the same thing: microwave ovens just don't cook some foods as well as regular ovens do. The reason why: because micro-waves cook by exciting the water molecules in food (see the previous question), the food inside a micro-wave oven rarely cooks at temperatures higher than 212°F, the temperature at which water turns to steam. Conventional ovens, on the other hand, cook at tem-peratures as high as 550°F. High temperatures are needed to caramelize sugars and break down proteins, carbohydrates, and other substances and combine them into more complex flavors. Microwave ovens can't do any of this, and they can't bake, either.

PUT A FORK IN IT

Q: Why can't you put metal in a microwave?

A: If you've ever put a fork into a microwave by accident, then you've no doubt seen the sparks—and possibly even destroyed your microwave. (If you've ever done this on purpose, seek professional help.)

It's not that metal in a microwave automatically means damage. As you learned on the previous page, the interior walls of microwave ovens are made of metal, as is the mesh on the glass door. The holes in the mesh are large enough to let out visible light (which has a small wavelength), but too small to allow the microwaves (which have a larger wavelength) to escape. So you can see what's cooking without getting cooked yourself. (This is called a Faraday cage.)

And you can put metal in a microwave in certain situations. If you've ever cooked a frozen pizza on a shiny cardboard stand, or a Hot Pocket that goes in a shiny cardboard pouch, that shine is made of aluminum…a kind of metal.

So what is it about a fork that makes it kill microwave ovens? Its shape. The metal walls are flat, and so is the aluminum lining that a Hot Pocket or frozen pizza is cooked in. When microwaves hit water, ceramic, or plastic, they are absorbed. But metal has free-moving electrons, which don't absorb microwaves. Instead, the microwaves make them move faster. Those excited electrons will heat up a flat metal surface—that's why frozen food products can be cooked in carefully tested aluminum lining; they will heat your pizza faster because the flat surface disperses the heat evenly.

But a fork does not have a flat surface, so all of those excited electrons have nowhere to go but up to the top of the tines, which become too crowded and begin to arc, setting off sparks. Let the microwave go for too long and the tips of the tines will actually burn off. The oven's interior walls can even burn up, destroying the magnetron. Spoons are a little bit safer than forks, but it's still not a good idea to put them—or any metal, such as a bowl with a metal lining—in the microwave.

BYE-BYE, BALLOON

Q: Why do balloons slowly deflate?

Q: As the thin wall of rubber stretches to inflate, the surface becomes so thin that microscopic holes result. Air molecules are able to slowly escape through them. This slow leakage is even faster when it comes to helium-filled mylar balloons. That's because helium exists as a single atom, so it's smaller and quicker. That air you breathed into the balloon bonds as two or three atoms (and of different elements, including carbon dioxide). Those elements can clog up the tiny holes. But either way, your balloon's days are numbered.

GEOGRAPHY

THE ALOHA PARADOX

Q: Why does Hawaii have interstate highways?

A: It seems quite silly that the state of Hawaii, which consists of several islands located more than 2,400 miles away from the U.S. mainland, would be part of the country's interstate highway system. But the name is something of a misnomer—if you ignore the capitalization, that is. Hawaii isn't part of *an* interstate system, it's part of *the* Interstate system. That's an official designation that means it's controlled by the federal government and receives federal funding. Specifically, Hawaii's highways fall under the jurisdiction of the Dwight D. Eisenhower System of Interstate and National Defense Highways, built in the 1950s to speedily get supplies from military base to military base in the event of foreign attack. That makes sense, considering the last U.S. military base to be bombed by a foreign country was Hawaii's Pearl Harbor in 1941.

TWISTED TWISTERS

Q: Why is it that tornadoes always seem to hit trailer parks?

A: Conventional wisdom has always held that the reason why twisters pick up and throw trailers is because twisters are so powerful that they have to pick up something… and because trailers aren't secured to the ground like permanent structures, they get tossed around.

But in 2014, researchers at Indiana's Purdue University (located in the heart of Tornado Alley) may have found the science behind the phenomenon. After studying 60 years of data collected by the National Weather Service's Storm Prediction Center unit, the scientists noticed a commonality: tornadoes most often touch down in what are called "transition zones." These are areas where a dramatic geographic or landscape change occurs. Examples of transition zones include where a forest ends and the plains begin, or in the case of tornadoes, where cities end and turn into sparsely populated flat land. That just so happens to be where most mobile home parks exist.

N-E-W-S BREAK

Q: **Where did the cardinal directions come from, and why a cardinal?**

A: The four main points that make up the cardinal directions—north, south, east, and west—have been used by explorers (and the hopelessly lost) for thousands of years. Several world cultures developed their own versions. These Latin terms, used by the ancient Romans, might sound a bit familiar: *borealis* for north, *orientalis* for east, *australis* for south, and *occidentalis* for west.

However, those words failed to take hold after the fall of the Roman Empire. Instead, it was the Germanic words for the directions that found their way into the Romance languages: the Proto-Germanic *norþ* meant "to the left of the rising sun." East comes from *aus-t*, "dawn"; south, from *sunþ*, "seethe, boil" (this is also where the word "sun" came from); and west comes from *wes-t*, which meant "evening."

As for the term "cardinal directions," it has nothing to do with the bird or the Catholic religious leader—it was derived from an old definition of "cardinal" in the 14th century, which meant "pivotal, chief, or essential."
Bonus Fact: Contrary to popular belief, the word "news" is not an acronym for "north, east, west, and south" (as in, "What's happening in the news?"). The word entered Middle English in the 14th century as *new*, from the Old French *nouveau*. That gave us the words "new" and "news," the latter word a rare "plural adjective," which turned it into a noun, as in, "A lot of new things are news."

ARE WE THERE YET?

Q: **When a highway mileage sign says "New York City 34 Miles Ahead"—is that to the border, to the first exit within the city, or to the middle of the city?**

A: The answer: none of those things, or at least not necessarily. The Federal Highway Administration has given the "control cities" listed on these mileage signs a "center point." The criteria for a center point: whatever the local authorities want it to be. It could literally be anything, so long as the FHA approves it as a "well-defined central area." That could be a downtown, a central business district, or city hall, for example. Mileage signs leading into Baltimore denote how far away City Hall is.

In New York City, the distance measures to the busy Columbus Circle area in Manhattan.

THE BIG APPLE JUICE

Q: Why are water towers and tanks so common on the rooftops of New York City buildings?

A: If you haven't noticed these ubiquitous water towers, you will the next time you visit New York City, or see it depicted on-screen (provided the show or movie was actually filmed there). In the late 19th century, a law was passed that all of the city's buildings over six stories must provide enough individual water storage so people on the upper floors have decent water pressure. It also helps to put out fires that start above the sixth floor. Aqueducts and water pressure can take care of the first six floors; the amount of extra water and the size of the tank are commensurate with the number of extra floors.

ALL WET

Q: What's the difference between an ocean and a sea?

A: The definition of oceans: "continuous bodies of salt-water surrounding the continents," which technically means there's only one, because they all connect. However, if all of the ocean water were removed from the Earth, the continents would be surrounded by deep depressions, each of which is considered an ocean.

These are the Atlantic, the Pacific, the Arctic, the Indian, and the Southern.

Now to seas. Despite the old adage, there are a lot more than seven of them. (The "seven seas" phrase came from splitting up the Atlantic and the Pacific Oceans into North and South, which makes for seven seas when you add the other three.)

When it comes to actual seas, geographers say there are about 50. What makes a sea a sea? They are usually shallower areas that differ from the surrounding ocean in some way—physically, chemically, or biologically. For example, the Caribbean Sea is a part of the Atlantic Ocean, but its waters are much clearer and have a lower salt content.

SALT OF THE EARTH

Q: Does anything live in the Dead Sea?

A: The Dead Sea is actually a lake in the Middle East surrounded by Israel, Jordan, and a few other countries. The surface is 1,312 feet below sea level, making it the lowest point on the planet. It's also among the saltiest lakes on Earth. The Dead Sea's salinity (dissolved salt content) typically hovers around the 33 percent mark—that's about eight times saltier than the Pacific Ocean.

Needless to say, drinking a glass of water from the Dead Sea wouldn't be a very smart move (but its ability to make just about anything float is kind of fun). So, yes, the mega-high salt content precludes most animals from living in the Dead Sea. But not all animals; scientists have discovered a few microscopic organisms that thrive there, mostly tiny fungi and bacteria.

ANCIENT MISNOMER

Q: **Why is it called "Rhode Island" if it's not an island?**

A: Because it reminded Italian explorer Verrazzano, who landed there in 1524, of the Greek island of Rhodes.

SETTING THE STANDARD

Q: **Why are there time zones?**

A: Before the railroads, there were no time zones. Noon in any city was whenever the sun reached the meridian of that particular place. Time actually varied by one minute for every 13 miles traveled, and cities only a few hundred miles apart had different times, which made scheduling trains very difficult. For example, when it was noon in Chicago, it was 12:31 in Pittsburgh, 12:17 in Toledo, 11:50 in St. Louis, and 11:27 in Omaha. At one time, U.S. railroads had nearly 300 different time zones. This lack of consistency wasn't just inconvenient, it was dangerous. The possibility of train wrecks increased dramatically with the confusing schedules. Something had to be done—not locally, but on a global basis.

By 1847, Great Britain had a unified time system,

which meant it had a single time zone across the entire country. That was fine for the small island nation. But it wasn't as easy in North America—the United States and Canada cover some 60 degrees of longitude. In 1872 the Time-Table Convention was founded in St. Louis to look for a solution. Charles Dowd, a school principal from New York, recommended that the U.S. set up standard time zones, and brought his idea to Congress. Most lawmakers agreed with the idea, but were afraid it would upset their constituents, so the bill was stalled on the House floor for more than a decade.

It wasn't until Sir Sandford Fleming, a well-respected Canadian railroad engineer, brought a specific solution to an international time conference that the idea began to take hold. His idea: because there are 24 hours in a day, divide the Earth's 360 degrees by 24, which will create 24 equal time zones separated by 15 degrees.

In 1882, the Standard Time system was finally adopted, officially dividing the United States into four time zones—Eastern, Central, Mountain, and Pacific. At noon on Sunday, November 18, 1883—a day that became known as "the day with two noons"—the railroads set their clocks to this new system.

HISTORY

BRIDGE OVER TROUBLED WATERS

Q: **Did London Bridge really ever fall down, like in the nursery rhyme?**

A: Yes, lots of times. The bridge over the river Thames in London began its storied life as a wooden structure built by the Romans in A.D. 55. After the Roman Empire fell and various factions (including the Vikings) invaded Britain during the Dark Ages, the bridge was neglected and fell down quite a few times until it was fortified in stone in 1176.

For the next 300 years, London Bridge was a bustling little village in its own right. Thousands of people passed over and under it each day, lived inside homes that were built on top of it, worshipped in its churches, and shopped in its 130 shoppes. During that time, the heads of England's slain enemies—including, most famously, William Wallace and Thomas More—were displayed on the Stone Gateway on the bridge's southern end. After a while, it became so crowded that a separate bridge was erected nearby for pedestrians who needed to get over the river quickly. The nursery rhyme was based on earlier, similar songs from elsewhere in Europe. The first English version was written in the 1630s.

But London Bridge had a few more falls to come.

After nearly sinking into the Thames because the foundation couldn't support all of the weight, the bridge was razed and rebuilt yet again in 1831. (The first ship to pass underneath it was the HMS *Beagle*, later made famous by the explorations of Charles Darwin.)

London Bridge was replaced again in the 1920s, and yet again in 1962 after an American named Robert McCulloch purchased the old one for $2.5 million and moved it piece by piece to Lake Havasu City in Arizona (*Guinness World Records* lists it as the "world's largest antique"). A new London Bridge was built in 1973 out of steel and concrete. And in the 2016 action movie *London Has Fallen*, London Bridge falls down yet again…after it gets blown up.

Bonus Fact: Why is the river Thames pronounced "tems"? The first known reference comes from the Celtic word *Tamïssa*, meaning "dark river." In Latin it became *Tamesis* and then in Middle English, *Temese*. The "h" was added during the Renaissance, possibly as an homage to the Thyamis River in Greece, but the pronunciation of the hard "T" remained.

LIGHT ONE CANDLE

Q: Exactly how "dark" were the Dark Ages?

A: Most history books mark the beginning of the Dark Ages to A.D. 476, when the Germanic leader Odoacer overthrew the Roman emperor Romulus and became king of Italy. That marked the end of the Roman Empire and the beginning of a period in Europe in which nothing good happened to anyone at all for several centuries. Okay, that's an exaggeration, but it was a period in Europe during which plagues were commonplace and technological advancements weren't.

The mood wouldn't "lighten up" again until the European Renaissance began in the 14th century. That's when the Dark Ages was given its name, coined by the Italian poet Petrarch in the 1330s; he wrote that people from that age were "surrounded by darkness and dense gloom."

Modern historians, however, think that Petrarch's assessment was a bit too gloomy. Many don't even use the term "Dark Ages," instead preferring to call it the Middle Ages or the Migration Period.

It's not that the Dark Ages weren't a bleak time in Europe—they were—but they weren't *that* bad. Consider the facts: military conflicts during this period weren't nearly as destructive as those staged by Rome's armies. Major advancements, including the creation of Carolingian minuscule, a standardized form of handwriting, greatly sped up the process of bookmaking. And—not counting all the plagues—the standards of living were actually pretty high when compared to most of human history prior to that. Best of all, peasants and commoners alike had plenty of access to cheap beer. (Did they prefer dark ale?)

SETTING THE BAR LOW

Q: Who did people exaggeratively say their foes were "worse than" before Hitler?

A: When someone is called "worse than Hitler," they're being compared to the monster who tried to conquer a continent and, in doing so, killed six million people based solely on their faith. Although that might sound like an unfair comparison (for most people), dropping the "H-bomb" on a rival has become commonplace.

And it's certainly not a new thing. The concept of exaggerating somebody else's misdeeds through comparison to history's worst villains far predates the Third Reich. Before then, anyone looking to thoroughly shame an opponent would compare them to a villain from the Bible. Judas, the apostle who betrayed Jesus, was a frequent example, as was Pontius Pilate, the Roman judge who sentenced Jesus to death.

But no biblical bad guy was invoked more than the Pharaoh; in Exodus he refused to free the Hebrew slaves and instead rained ten plagues down upon them. That will get you a lot of bad press. For example, in Thomas Paine's 1776 Revolutionary War–fueling pamphlet "Common Sense," he refers to King George III as "the hardened, sullen tempered Pharaoh of England." (Paine then added, "In another 150 years or so, George will be even worse than Hitler!")

WHO STANDS LIKE THAT?

Q: Why did people in old portraits pose with their hands inside their waistcoats?

A: It's a pose most associated with a famous portrait of French emperor Napoleon Bonaparte: he stands regally, one arm at his side and the other slightly tucked into the front lapel of his waistcoat (what Americans would call a vest). For years, people have wondered why the emperor's hand was hiding in his pocket. Did the artist not know how to paint hands? Did Napoleon have a stomach ulcer that was bothering him? Was he simply winding his watch? Or was he trying to hide his *horribly deformed hand*!? Answer: none of the above.

This was actually a common pose for men of elevated status, but by the time Napoleon used it in the 1800s, it was already on the way out. The 1738 *Book of Genteel Behavior* suggested the pose displayed "manly boldness tempered with modesty," as if the subject could go for a concealed weapon...but doesn't. Ancient Greek and Roman leaders used the pose, as did European leaders of the 1700s. Napoleon, in turn, was emulating all of them.

A more practical reason for the hand-in-the-pocket pose: it was comfortable. Sitting or standing for a portrait, and later a daguerreotype, took a long time. Keeping one hand in a breast pocket helped the subject stay relaxed and not move around too much. It was for this same reason that subjects in old paintings and photographs rarely smiled.

SHORT-CHANGED

Q: Was Napoleon really that short?

A: No. Napoleon stood 5 feet 6½ inches tall: a bit short by today's standards—but not by the standards of his time. The average height of a Parisian man circa 1800 was about 5 feet 6 inches, which made Napoleon a bit above average in height. So why does the world think of him as short?

Here's one theory: the men he was most often seen with—the *grenadiers* of his Imperial Guard—were very tall. That might have started the rumor, and it might be why English political cartoons depicted him as short. But that's not the answer.

After Napoleon died in 1821, the coroner measured his body using the old French system called *pieds de roi*, which translates to "feet of the king." So his height was listed as 5 feet 2 inches. If the coroner had used the English system, Napoleon would have been 4½ inches taller. But the British didn't know that the old French measurement was used. Result: one of history's greatest military leaders is still thought of as a short man with a "Napoleon complex"…because of a simple conversion error.

HEADS UP

Q: Why were Washington, Jefferson, Lincoln, and Teddy Roosevelt chosen for Mount Rushmore?

A: In the 1920s, the state of South Dakota needed a tourism boost. State historian Doane Robinson had an idea: turn one of the state's most impressive geological features—a set of huge granite spires called the Needles—into a massive sculpture depicting famous American heads.

But there were several problems with the Needles: local American Indians considered them sacred, and environmentalists and outdoor lovers worried that the sculpture would destroy their natural beauty. Even worse: the man who was hired to sculpt the monument, Gutzon Borglum, informed Robinson that the granite was so weak that the heads would need to be very small. With that, the Needles were out.

So a search commenced for a second site. That's when they found nearby Mount Rushmore, a granite cliff large enough to easily fit four giant heads.

But which heads? South Dakota lawmakers debated all sorts of ideas, form explorers such as Lewis and Clark, to Wild West legend Buffalo Bill Cody. Borglum, the artist, thought it should be presidents, and he was able to convince the project organizers.

But which presidents? Everyone agreed that George Washington should be included. Choosing the remaining three proved more difficult.

The current president, Calvin Coolidge, insisted that the remainders consist of two Republicans and one Democrat (Coolidge was a Republican). Thomas Jefferson was chosen for his role in crafting the Declaration of Independence, and Abraham Lincoln for his role during the Civil War. The final selection, Theodore Roosevelt, was a bit more controversial. Detractors pointed to his bombastic character and recent time in office as reasons to choose another president. But his Republican status, plus the fact that he was awarded a Nobel Peace Prize, helped Roosevelt earn the final spot. Construction began on the slopes of Mount Rushmore in 1927 and was completed in 1941.

And the plan to boost tourism certainly worked.

Today, Mount Rushmore National Memorial receives more than 2.1 million visitors a year, making it the most popular roadside attraction in South Dakota by far.

SOME QUESTIONS HAVE NO ANSWERS

"Why do people say, 'It was more fun than a barrel of monkeys'? Have you ever *smelled* a barrel of monkeys?"

—STEVE BLUESTEIN

THE TAME WEST

Q: **Was the "Wild West" really as violent as it's been portrayed in the movies?**

A: Based on what Hollywood has shown us, you'd think that everyone in the American West was either shooting someone or running away from someone who was trying to shoot them. As Clint Eastwood put it in 1963's *The Good, The Bad and the Ugly*: "In this world there's two kinds of people, my friend: those with loaded guns and those who dig. You dig."

Was it really a violent, lawless wasteland where murder and gunfights occurred every day? No. During the heyday of the Old West (roughly 1870–85), the five major towns of Dodge City, Ellsworth, Caldwell, Abilene, and Wichita had a combined total of 45 murders. That's a rate of one per 100,000 residents. The 2014 murder rate in the United States was 4.5 per 100,000 residents. That's more than four times as dangerous as the "Wild" West.

OFFSHORE ACCOUNTS

Q: Did pirates really bury their treasure?

A: Wouldn't it make more sense for a pirate to sail to the nearest safe port, hand over a portion of the treasure to the crew, and start spending the remainder like there's no tomorrow? That's what most of them did during the golden age of piracy (roughly the 16th to the 18th centuries). But what if there was no safe port, or the pirate didn't trust his fellow shipmates? That's why many of them preferred to bury their loot—or leave it in other secret locations—until it could be retrieved when the coast was clear.

However, hiding ill-gotten gains didn't always work out. For example, Sir Francis Drake and his men robbed a Spanish mule train loaded with silver and gold in 1573. They made off with 20 tons and decided to bury most of it because they couldn't carry it all back to their boats. Unfortunately, they didn't hide it well enough, and the Spanish managed to retrieve it.

Other pirates, including Roche Brasiliano and Captain William Kidd, suffered even worse fates. Brasiliano was tortured by Spanish soldiers until he revealed the location of his hidden stash, as did Kidd after he was captured in Boston in 1699.

THIS QUESTION IS RATED ARRRRR!

Q: **Did real pirates talk with the hard "r" sound and say stuff like "Avast, me hearties"?**

A: There was no distinct pirate accent when pirates ruled the seas. Why? Because they came from all over Europe, Asia, Africa, and beyond. The pirate dialect we know of today can be traced back to a few Hollywood movies from the 1950s, including *Blackbeard the Pirate* and *Long John Silver*. Both famous pirates were played by British character actor Robert Newton, who spoke in a West Country English accent.

In most other parts of England, the "r" sound is diminished (it sounds more like "ah"), but not in the west. There, they pronounce their "r"s hard, and they tend to replace "is" and "are" with "be"; they even say "arr" in the place of "yes."

For his portrayal as Long John Silver, Newton exaggerated this speaking style to give his character more verve. Newton did it so well that later actors who played pirates emulated him, and before long, that's how everyone thought pirates talked. So when someone tells you to talk like a pirate on Talk Like a Pirate Day, just do your best Robert Newton impression.

FROZEN IN TIME

Q: **Did a comet really wipe out all of the dinosaurs?**

A: Not quite. No one knows exactly what put an end to the dinosaurs' reign, but it was most likely a multitude of factors. In recent years, scientists have speculated that the six-mile-wide comet (or possibly an asteroid) that slammed into Mexico's Yucatán Peninsula 66 million years ago only served as a death blow for the dinosaurs, which were already on their way out.

In the years leading up to the strike, several massive volcanic eruptions in Asia helped contribute to catastrophic climate change. As temperatures across the planet dropped, the dinosaurs' cold-blooded physiology couldn't handle the frigid weather. They started dying off in swarms. Some scientists theorize that all nonavian dinosaurs died out before the comet even arrived.

However, no one knows exactly *when* the volcanoes blew their tops. A team of geoscientists at the University of California–Berkeley posit that the comet's strike may have been so massive that it actually kickstarted the volcanoes. Major earthquakes, while not as powerful as a comet strike, have been known to cause volcanic eruptions. A 9.5 magnitude quake that struck Chile in 1960 caused a few volcanoes to erupt in the Andes.

Regardless of how it all went down, the one-two punch of the comet and the eruptions spelled doom for the dinosaurs. Both incidents kicked up tons of dust and carbon dioxide that blotted out the sun, dropped the Earth's average temperature, and sent the reigning reptiles to a frozen grave.

WILD
ANIMALS

COOL IT

Q: Why do elephants have such big ears?

A: If you said "to hear better," you'd be only partially correct. The primary function of these massive body parts, which can reach five feet in diameter in African elephants, is to cool down the animal. The thin ears contain thousands of tiny blood vessels. On hot days, an elephant fans its ears, but it's not the whoosh of air on the rest of the body that does most of the cooling; it's the air passing over the thin skin of the ears, which cools the blood vessels within by as much as 10°F. As the cooler blood flows into the rest of the animal, it keeps the elephant from overheating. Neat trick.

NUMSKULLS

Q: Why don't woodpeckers get headaches?

A: If you tried slamming your face against a maple tree 20 times per second with the same force that a woodpecker uses, you probably wouldn't survive the attempt. (If you do survive, the Avengers could always use some more help.) The woodpecker's biology is definitely superhero material; its head can absorb a lot of force—between 600 and 1,200 g's. To put that in perspective, 1 g (short for g-force) is the equivalent to the pressure applied to the human body by the gravitational constant at sea level. Most people will pass out when they hit 4 or 5 g's.

So what's Woody Woodpecker's secret? Thanks to the bird's anatomy, all of that force is not absorbed by the brain case. Instead, it goes through the upper jaw, which allows the force to dissipate through the rest of the body. But that's not all: the woodpecker also has a special bone called a *hyoid* that surrounds the skull, keeping it in place like a seat belt. Finally, the brain is packed snugly inside the skull, giving it no room to bounce around during all that pecking, like a motorcycle helmet. Result: no headaches.

FOR CRYING OUT LOUD!

Q: Can an elephant cry crocodile tears?

A: The concept of crocodile tears goes all the way back to antiquity. It stems from the simple biological fact that the reptile's lacrimal glands produce a fluid that is secreted behind the nictitating membrane to keep the eyes moist and free of bacteria while on land. When ancient people observed the crocodile "crying" as it callously ate its prey, the reptile got a reputation as a cold-hearted killer that sheds empty tears. Over time, that trait came to describe callous people who pretended to feel bad about something; they were said to be crying "crocodile tears." The ancient Greeks mentioned the phrase, as did several later writers, including Shakespeare: "Oh, devil, devil! If that the earth could teem with woman's tears, Each drop she falls would prove a crocodile." (*Othello*—Act 4, Scene 1) And it's still in use today.

So back to the original question: Do elephants cry crocodile tears? No, elephants cry elephant tears. And unlike the cold-blooded crocs, elephants can also cry emotional tears.

HEY, THAT'S THE TITLE OF THE BOOK!

Q: **Do geese get goose bumps?**

A: Geese do get goose bumps, but not the kind that you get. The term comes from the appearance of a goose's skin after it's been plucked. The feathers of geese and other fowl grow out of stores in the skin that resemble hair follicles, so after the feathers are gone, it looks, well, bumpy.

When it comes to human goose bumps, the scientific name is *cutis anserina*, and the reflex of producing it is known as *piloerection*, the *pilomotor reflex*, or *horripilation* (that's the same root that gives us the word "horror"). The condition occurs whenever you get very scared, cold, or sexually aroused. But this condition only affects mammals, not birds, fish, reptiles, or invertebrates—all of which have other methods for keeping warm and scaring off predators.

This involuntary behavior predates modern humans to a time when our ancestors were covered in hair. When they got cold or scared, their hairs bristled—either to make them warmer, or to make them appear larger. All mammals do this—the most dramatic example is the porcupine. When a porcupine gets goose bumps, you want to be far, far away.

Bonus Fact: The term is cross-cultural; the Germans, Swedish, and Danish also get "goose bumps." The Dutch get "chicken bumps," and the Hebrew term translates to "duck skin."

BETTER THAN PLAID

Q: Why do tigers have stripes?

A: As Frosted Flakes spokescat Tony the Tiger might put it: "It's because stripes are gr-r-reat!" He's right—they give these feline predators an evolutionary advantage.

Tigers didn't always have stripes; they developed over the course of thousands of years. Their function: to keep the tiger camouflaged while hunting. Considering that adult male tigers can weigh up to 670 pounds, they have to eat lots of meat in order to survive. That means fooling their keen-eyed, fast-footed prey. Why orange and black? Zoologists say that the orange hair helps tigers blend in with grass and underbrush while the black stripes break up the color, thus making a tiger on the prowl more difficult to spot.

Another stripy animal: the zebra. Technically, they are white with black stripes, not the other way around. And just as tigers use their stripes to fool prey, zebras use theirs to fool predators—from large lions to tiny tsetse flies. Thanks to the stripes, predators can't tell where one zebra begins and the other ends. Interestingly, zebras are instinctively attracted to anything with black and white stripes. Even if stripes are painted on a wall, a zebra will go stand next to them!

INSIDE OUT

Q: What is a turtle shell?

A: The turtle's shell is technically part of its skeleton—the ribs and backbones, to be exact. The shells get their distinctive patterns not from the bones but from the *scutes* on top of the bones, which are made of *keratin* (the primary substance in hair, nails, and hooves in other animals). Although the turtle's upper shell, called the *carapace*, is hard enough to withstand attacks from most predators, it is very sensitive to the touch. (In fact, some turtles like to be petted. However, do not attempt to pet a snapping turtle.)

THE HUDDLED MASSES

Q: How do penguins stay warm in the coldest place on Earth?

A: In the frigid tundra of Antarctica, winter temperatures can plummet below -80°F. The penguin's success in this harsh environment can be credited to both biology and behavior.

First, the biology: compared to most other birds, Adélie and emperor penguins are quite large, and their volume ratio, along with their feathers and protective layers of fat, helps the birds retain heat. However, two penguin body parts are not insulated: their feet and flippers. Fortunately, evolution has provided a solution. The muscles they use for swimming and walking are located in the warmer regions of their bodies. Their feet and flippers aren't as affected by the cold because they're mostly comprised of bone and tendons. And penguins' black feathers help retain heat from sunlight.

But biology alone isn't enough, so behavior plays a key role: because it can get so cold inland, penguins spend most of their time near the coastline, where it's somewhat warmer (but still colder than most humans are comfortable with). Massing along the coast also provides them with convenient access to fish in the Southern Ocean. And when it's *really* cold, penguins huddle together in large groups. Body heat keeps the birds on the inside warm, and the more robust birds take shifts on the outside of the huddle—where winds can reach 70 mph.

SOME QUESTIONS HAVE NO ANSWERS

"Did you ever notice that people who say they don't care what other people think are usually desperate to have people think they don't care what people think?"

—GEORGE CARLIN

A VIEW TO A KRILL

Q: Why do blue whales grow so large?

A: The blue whale is the world's largest animal—it can weigh more than 200 tons and grow as long as a basketball court. It's amazing that it gets this big considering it eats krill. The average weight of one of these tiny, shrimplike animals: less than 0.07 ounce.

So as you might imagine, a blue whale has to eat a lot of krill. How much? Up to four tons *every day*. Biologists theorize that blue whales became this large in order stay warm in the world's oceans. All that blubber keeps them toasty and safe from predators. Their aquatic environment is also more "fat friendly" than land. Buoyancy enables them to grow increasingly large, and an ocean full of krill keeps them very well fed.

UNDER PRESSURE

Q: How do deep-sea creatures avoid getting the bends?

A: Deep-sea divers know the risks all too well: descend too deep below the surface and the immense weight of the water will cause air bubbles to form inside their bodies. If the diver swims back up to the surface too quickly, those bubbles can cause serious damage. This is typically called "the bends," but it's also known as decompression sickness. At the very least, it causes severe joint pain; at the worst, paralysis, or even death.

Deep-diving dolphins, whales, and seals can cope with the intense pressure changes thanks to collapsible lungs that allow them to take shorter breaths more often in order to safely continue their treks. Deep-sea fish, on the other hand, have developed pressure levels within their bodies that help keep them from getting squished. If they were to float to higher waters, however, they would get slammed with a nasty case of the bends. A quick swim to the surface would, in many cases, cause these fish to explode.

THE FAB FOUR-TRILLION

Q: Which type of animal is there the most of in the world?

A: There are more than seven billion humans on Earth, but we have a long way to go if we want to pass insects for the title "Most Populous Living Organism on the Planet." Overlooking bacteria and other microscopic critters, there are so many bugs on the planet that it's difficult for most people to comprehend: for every one of us, there are 200 million of them.

But which insect wins the numbers game? Famed evolutionary biologist J. B. S. Haldane put it this way: "God has an inordinate fondness for beetles." There are more beetle species—about 380,000—than any other animal. Forty percent of all insects are beetles. They account for about 25 percent of all known life-forms on Earth.

Beetles have been around since before the dinosaurs because they're tough to kill (thanks to their armored shells) and are highly adaptive. Consider that the ladybug and firefly are both beetles, as is the Goliath beetle, which can grow larger than your hand.

HOMEWRECKERS

Q: How and why do termites eat wood?

A: So tiny and yet so destructive, the average worker termite is less than one centimeter long, but it sports one of nature's toughest mandibles. This may seem a bit odd considering that termites are *detritivores*, organisms that feed on dead and decomposing organic matter. But in their continuing quest for food, termites have developed the ability eat just about any dead plant material—and wood is one of their favorite meals. Once they find it, they don't stop eating until it's gone— they barely even sleep.

A single termite nest can make mincemeat out of your house, furniture, and even books. That's why a home with a termite infestation is often a total loss. By the time the homeowner finds out, it's usually too late.

Not all species of termites are pests, though. Many prefer to stick to rural areas and eat grass, leaves, and other plant matter. And they provide a valuable source of food to people and livestock in impoverished regions of the world. Believe it or not, per pound, termites are packed with more protein than beef.

COUNT BATULA

Q: Do vampire bats really drink blood?

A: At least three species of bats (out of 1,200) depend on blood for sustenance: the white-winged vampire bat, the hairy-legged vampire bat, and the common vampire bat—all native to Central and South America. In fact, they're the only mammals that live on blood alone.

Most of these bats prefer to suck the blood from sleeping mammals, primarily horses and cattle, but they've also been known to attack birds. They sneak up on their targets on foot and then use their keen sense of *thermoception*, which detects an ideal "hot spot" on their victim's body that's chock-full of blood. Vampire bats can feed for up to 30 minutes. If their victim wakes up, the bat will utilize its springy forelimbs to quickly take off vertically and fly away much in the same manner as a Harrier jump jet.

Vampire bats use their sharp teeth to shave off fur or feathers, and then use their incisors to cut into their victim's skin and suck out the blood. Although their bites are rarely deadly, vampire bats can cause infections and sometimes diseases. In a few very rare cases, they've transmitted rabies to humans. While they rarely target people, a colony of 100 vampire bats can drink the blood of 25 cows in a single year.

Bonus Fact: If the world's only blood-eating bats live in the Americas, then how come vampires are a European legend? Stories of vampires go back to a time long before Europeans knew of vampire bats. But after explorers returned from expeditions to the Americas in the early 18th century, they brought scary stories—related to them by the natives—of bats that came in the night and sucked their slumbering victims' blood, some of whom became infected with rabies and acted strangely. Before long, all bats became feared as bloodsuckers.

BUSY AS A BEE

Q: How many bees does it take to make enough honey to fill one cup?

A: Honeybees are among the animal kingdom's most industrious and hardworking creatures. Young females are tasked with serving as nurses for developing larvae. Then, when they reach a certain age, they take their first few test flights before zooming out of their hives in search of pollen.

The bees often toil from dawn until dusk (which helps explain their short six-week life span). What does all that hard work add up to? Not much. The average worker bee produces about a twelfth of a teaspoon of honey in her lifetime.

That's right, "her." Only female honeybees actually work. Their male counterparts, typically called "drones," are born without stingers, and the only thing they do is mate. While that might sound like a pretty good gig, many of these defenseless drones are shoved out of the hive and left to die when wintertime comes and food is scarce.

To answer the original question, it would take 576 worker bees their entire lifetimes to fill a single cup with honey.

BEE-N NICE KNOWING YOU

Q: What would happen if all of the world's honeybees died?

A: If pollinating bees all kick the honeybucket, it's not only bad news for humans but for most of the world's plants and animals. Since the year 2000, millions of these hardworking insects have disappeared under mysterious circumstances. Scientists call this phenomenon "colony collapse disorder," which involves worker bees abruptly vanishing, leaving their queen and a handful of their colleagues all alone to fend for themselves.

Biologists aren't exactly sure why this is happening, but they've narrowed down the possible culprits to a lethal combination of parasitic flies, pesticides, and electromagnetic interference. Put them all together, and it causes the bees to become disoriented and incapable of finding their way back to their hives.

If this scenario continues to worsen, the world's plants will stop getting pollinated, causing a chain reaction all the way up the food chain. In human terms, the worst-case scenario is that millions of crops will die, devastating not just farmers and the impoverished, but sending the world's economy into uncharted waters.

Thankfully, it probably won't come to that. While bugs aid about one-third of humanity's crops—and bees handle the bulk of the workload—there are other insects whose numbers could be boosted in the case of a bee catastrophe. And scientists are fervently working on methods to artificially pollinate crops. Expect to hear a lot more about this problem in the coming years.

PRETTY IN PINK

Q: Why are flamingos pink?

A: They aren't always pink. Young flamingos have gray plumage, and an adult flamingo can be white, orange, red, or pink. The water bird's coloring depends on its habitat and food. Flamingos live at the edge of very salty lagoons (they can even drink salt water, excreting the salt through glands near their beaks) where they feed on brine shrimp and algae. These foods contain a high amount of *carotenoids*, the organic pigments that produce color in plants and animals. Brine shrimp and algae contain high amounts of a particular carotenoid called *canthaxanthin*, which turns things pink and orange. In the past, when zoo-keepers didn't know the secret of flamingo coloring, they didn't feed them the right carotenoids, and the birds were often white.

DOMESTICATED
ANIMALS

SMELL YA LATER

Q: **Why do dogs sniff each other's butts?**

A: You'd think that an animal with such a sophisticated sense of smell would avoid sticking its nose into the hindquarters of another (or its own). But *Canis lupus familiaris* has something else down there that you don't: anal sacs. These pouches contain glands that create odorous pheromones, scent molecules, and other secretions that help dogs get to know one another. It attracts them like magnets.

A single whiff can tell a dog a lot about the owner of the butt it's sniffing: its gender, age, diet, health, mood, and whether it might be a potential mate. This behavior also helps dogs establish hierarchy. A submissive dog will allow the sniffer to take all the time it needs; it will patiently wait its turn before doing the same. Dogs of the same temperament, size, and, more often than not, breed will take a few whiffs of each other's butts at the same time—kind of like a conference call.

HEAD OUT FOR A DRIVE

Q: **Why do dogs stick their heads out of the windows of moving cars?**

A: "Did you ever notice when you blow in a dog's face he gets mad at you," quipped comedian Steve Bluestone, "but when you take him in a car he sticks his head out the window?" There's actually a good reason for this odd behavior. But first, dogs don't like it when you blow in their face because it's annoying, and most animals (and humans, for that matter) would not enjoy such a thing. But when the dog gets into the car, it's a completely different scenario.

First and foremost, it's a very exciting activity. And the dog wants to add to that excitement by trying to take it all in. The wind rushing past his face is not unlike the sensation you get when you ride in a convertible. It's fun.

But there's more to it than that: When Fido sticks his head out of the window, he is looking around…with his nose. Dogs explore their environment with smell far more than they do with their other senses. In other words, they're "smelling the sights."

A TAIL TO TELL

Q: Why do dogs wag their tails?

A: Because they can't talk. No, really. Like butt-sniffing, tail-wagging is a form of communication—one that canines have been using since before they were domesticated. Coupled with specific postures and vocalizations, dogs have developed this language to directly convey emotions. A briskly wagging tail means the same thing a smile does for humans.

But wagging does not always equal happy. For example, a wag of just the tip of the tail might mean excitement. A slow wag conveys, "I'm happy, but I remain on alert, for you are a stranger." A tail held high says, "I'm dominant, so back off!" And when the tail is low and wagging, it means, "I am submissive" or "I am afraid."

One of the main reasons dogs communicate this way is because they can't see that well; it can be difficult for them to make out colors and detect facial expressions from a distance. And if the other dog is downwind, then their keen sense of smell is no help, either. But dogs' eyes are great at detecting movement (a trait that most predators share). So the tail wag is a way to communicate a lot of information from far away, letting the other dog know if it's safe to come closer. It's for this reason that several dog species have evolved big, bushy tails with white tips.

ALL DOG, NO BULL

Q: How in the world did we ever get the bulldog?

A: Bulldogs don't really make sense. They have breathing problems in general and small windpipes in particular. Their pups are often delivered by cesarean section because their heads were bred to be so big. They have poor eyesight, are very sensitive to the cold and heat, and they often suffer from hip and knee problems. They also have a penchant for attacking moving cars and vacuum cleaners. All of these odd traits can be traced back to the days when bulldogs used to bait bulls. Wait, what?

Bulldogs were specifically bred for a sport called bull-baiting, in which it was the dog's job to "take down" a bull by jumping up, biting its face, and hanging on until the bull was pinned to the ground. So the bulldog was bred to have a strong lower jaw and a less intrusive nose—that way, he can breathe while attacking the bull and then hang on indefinitely.

After bull-baiting was outlawed in the 19th century, the dog evolved into the shorter, squatter version we know today. Because of all that inbreeding, the bulldog's physique is terribly damaged and distorted. But unlike its barbaric ancestors, the modern bulldog is actually one of the more placid and generally happy breeds—a sweet companion with a constant case of the sniffles.

MAN'S TRUSTY FRIEND

Q: How did Fido become a generic name for dogs?

A: Does anyone name their dog Fido anymore? Not really. So many dogs, perhaps millions, were bestowed with that moniker over the past century and a half that today, "Fido" is simply a generic term for "dog." The name goes all the way back to ancient Rome, where it basically meant "trusty" in Latin. Its modern popularity, however, can be traced to a beloved 19th-century celebrity who named his dog Fido. That celebrity: Abraham Lincoln.

As a young lawyer in Illinois, Lincoln was battling depression, and keeping lots of animals around helped him cope. In 1855, he took in a stray mutt, a mustard-colored Lab mix that he named Fido, and the two were virtually inseparable for the next five years. That all changed when Lincoln won the White House and had to move his family to Washington, D.C. One of his first big executive decisions as president-elect: what to do with Fido. The dog did not like loud noises, and Lincoln feared the train ride might kill him. So reluctantly, despite the protests of his young sons Tad and Willy, the president left Fido with a family friend.

To ease the boys' pain (and no doubt his own), Lincoln arranged for Fido to sit for a series of photographs. Because Lincoln was such a beloved public figure (in the North, anyway), people wanted to know all about him. So, just as it is today, the press was happy to oblige. Result: the Fido prints were published in several magazines. The dog became one of the first animal celebrities in American history. By the time Lincoln was assassinated in 1865, the most common dog name in the country was Fido.

BARK! BARK! BARK!

Q: Why do dogs bark so much, and what are they saying?

A: Before dogs were domesticated, their wolf ancestors hung out on the outskirts of human settlements scavenging for scraps. Eventually they were taken in by humans and then bred to be more docile. In the process, they became more like puppies. In the wild, adult wolves don't really play, but most adult dogs love to play. That's the puppy in them. It also explains all that incessant barking. Puppies vocalize a lot more than mature canines, so one of the trade-offs of breeding dogs to be more puppylike is that they'll bark at anything—a passing car, the mailman, their own tail, etc. It's thrilling…not unlike a babbling toddler who babbles solely to hear his own voice.

POOPER-SCOOPER

Q: Who cleans up after Seeing-Eye dogs?

A: The people who actually walk the Seeing-Eye dogs, that's who. These amazing canines are trained from puppyhood to help their vision-impaired owners navigate through life. And part of their training is potty-related. The dogs are taught to go to the bathroom only when given a certain command. When that happens, their owner will run their hand down the dog's back to determine if it's #1 or #2. (The latter features a more arched back.) Once the deed is done, it's not too difficult for the owner to smell the pile and then pick it up with a plastic bag.

FELINE FINE

Q: Why do cats lick their fur after you pet them?

A: Why do cats do any of things that they do? *Felis catus* really is a strange creature. What other animal can fall off a table and then pretend it did it on purpose (other than humans, of course)? But the licking behavior seems strange even for cats. They demand that you pet them, and then after you're done, they lick the fur that you just petted. Reason: even though Fluffy wanted your love and attention, she didn't want you to leave your human scent all over her, so she licks it off.

A cat's fur is attached, by way of its skin, to subcutaneous glands (right below the skin) that release each cat's unique pheromones: its personal scent. Although a gentle petting session doesn't activate those glands, it does leave the oils from your skin all over the cat. The cat knows how to lick its own fur in such a way that it activates its scent glands to emit pheromones, but first it has to get rid of yours. The fewer scents on a cat, the better—it shows the competition that it is strong enough not to get licked, so to speak.

SOME QUESTIONS HAVE NO ANSWERS

"If men can run the world, why can't they stop wearing neckties? How intelligent is it to start the day by tying a little noose around your neck?

—LINDA ELLERBEE

MEOW HEAR THIS

Q: Why do cats meow at people but rarely at each other?

A: Because we don't speak cat. They have to meow to let us know if they're hungry, or if they want to go out, or if they want to be petted. When adult cats communicate with each other, they use a complex form of body language to get their point across. We humans can't read most of these subtle cues, which forces the cat to basically "shout" what it wants...not unlike the way some people talk slowly and loudly to someone they consider to be less intelligent.

Of course, adult cats do vocalize to—or at—each other when they're about to fight. Those are more growls and hisses than meows, however. And there's another form of vocal communication that cats utilize that may the strangest of all. (See the next question.)

GOOD VIBRATIONS

Q: How and why do cats purr?

A: A purring kitty in your lap may be one of life's most simple pleasures (unless you hate cats—then it's horrifying). But purring is also one of the most mysterious and unique behaviors in the animal kingdom. In fact, biologists still aren't sure exactly how or why cats purr. Although purring is commonly acknowledged to be a sign of contentment, cats also do it when they're frightened, in pain, or have suffered trauma. (If it was just one or the other, it might be easier to figure out what biological advantage they obtain from purring.) It is no doubt also a form of communication, possibly signaling to another cat that it isn't an enemy, a willing-ness to mate, an "I'm all right" signal in times of danger, or simply a pleasurable release when being petted.

It's also uncertain what specific mechanism the cat uses to purr. The most likely culprit: the rapid vibration of the muscles in the larynx (voice box), which causes the glottis (the opening between the vocal cords) to open and close rapidly as the cat both inhales and exhales. It's controlled, experts say, by a unique "neural oscillator" area in cats' brains.

Another theory is that purring involves the hyoid apparatus, a collection of small bones in the neck that support the tongue and tongue muscles. The cat's breathing can make one or more of these bones vibrate, thereby causing purring.

Here's where this behavior gets really interesting: purring might go beyond mere communication—recent findings suggest that it can help the cats stay healthy and heal faster when they're injured. A cat's purr vibrates at a frequency known to promote bone growth. Purring can also aid in muscle and tendon regenera-tion, and ease breathing in times of stress. It can even act as a pain reliever. So maybe it's not just dumb luck that cats seemingly have nine lives; they really can survive higher falls than other creatures their size.

This could explain why cats developed the ability to purr in the first place. Because they evolved to remain inactive for long periods of time in order to conserve energy between hunts, the animals required a passive method to stimulate their bones and muscles. Enter the purr: a low-energy way for cats to keep themselves fit without having to be active for most of the day.

So whatever the purr actually is, chances are it's a lot more than just the cat saying, "I'm happy right now."

HIGH HORSE

Q: Why are horses measured in hands?

A: Throughout history, human body parts have often provided units of measurement. That's why one foot is roughly the length of one foot. Ancient Egyptian records in particular tend to specify heights in hands. Over time, horse owners adopted the hand-measurement technique, and today horses are still mostly measured in hands, although much of Europe (except for the United Kingdom) uses the metric system to measure a horse's length. A hand is equal to four inches.

A STUBBORN LOT

Q: What are the differences among donkeys, mules, and hinnies?

A: All three of these farm animals are members of the family Equidae (horses), but they represent several species. They can interbreed, but their offspring are usually sterile. Donkeys were probably domesticated around 3000 B.C. in Egypt. A mule is the offspring of a male donkey and a mare.

Mules can be used just like horses, though they have more stamina and leg strength. Mules' reputation for stubbornness is, for the most part, undeserved. They're actually very smart and are usually stubborn only when asked to do something they consider dangerous. A hinny is the opposite of a mule: the offspring of a stallion and a female donkey.

RANGE ROVERS

Q: **Why are there no wild cows?**

A: We're not talking about feral cows that wander away from ranches, but actual wild cows. They did exist at one time. Early humans called the animal an *aurochs* before they domesticated it about 10,500 years ago. These wild cows continued to roam European grasslands until the 17th century.

Although the research is ongoing, scientists believe the aurochs was the precursor to the modern cow, though the wild aurochs was much larger than its domestic counterpart. In 1627, a poacher on a hunting preserve near Warsaw, Poland, killed the last known wild aurochs.

POUND FOR POUND

Q: What's the difference between a pig and a hog?

A: It's all in the poundage. In the United States, any fully grown swine weighing less than 180 pounds is generally called a pig. Any swine heavier than that is called a hog. (This isn't a global rule: all British swine are simply "pigs.")

The U.S. has other specialized names for swine. Newborns are called *piglets* until they're weaned. After that, the animal is called a *shoat* or a *weaner*. A half-grown pig can be a *gilt* (female), a *boar* (uncastrated male over six months old), or a *barrow* (castrated male). Adult females are *sows*, uncastrated males are still called *boars*, and castrated males are *stags*. (After death, most farm swine get a new name—either *sausage*, *chops*, *ham*, or *bacon*.)

END PRODUCTS

Q: Why do chickens lay so many eggs?

A: Ever find a bird's nest in the springtime? There might be three to six eggs in there. That's nothing compared to what a modern chicken can produce. The ancestors of these fowl weren't known for their egg-laying skills; they produced about as many eggs as most other birds, but centuries of selective breeding by farmers—pairing robust egg-layers with big, strong roosters—has produced a much larger chicken that can lay a whole lot of eggs.

How many? Depending on conditions such as the weather, the time of year, their age, how much food they've had to eat, and their overall temperament, the average domesticated hen can lay one or two eggs per day—that's over 500 eggs in one year! By comparison, wild hens only produce an average of 10 to 15 eggs in a year.

When it comes to egg production among modern poultry, the hen stands beak and shoulders above the competition. But in the wild kingdom, when it comes to cranking out lots of eggs at once, nothing can compete with the female ostrich. Those big birds can lay up to 50 eggs every year...and the eggs are six inches long! **Bonus Fact:** The ostrich lays the largest egg in the avian order, but it's actually the smallest bird egg in relation to the size of the bird.

SOME QUESTIONS HAVE NO ANSWERS

"How come the dove gets to be the peace symbol? How about the pillow? It has more feathers than the dove, and it doesn't have that dangerous beak."

—JACK HANDEY

BORN (NOT) TO BE WILD

Q: **How come some animals can be domesticated, and some can't?**

A: A domesticated animal is one that has been bred over several generations to live alongside—and become dependent on—humans for survival. They are domesticated as work animals, food sources, or pets. And the modern versions bear little resemblance to their wild ancestors. All dogs are descendants of wild wolves, for example, but your Morkipoo was selectively bred to preserve its human-friendly qualities (like being housetrained) and to get rid of the undesirable ones (like attacking people as prey).

This is not the same thing as a tame animal, or one that has become so acclimated to humans that it isn't threatened and can even be taught to do tricks or act in movies. Bart, a Kodiak brown bear that appeared in *Legends of the Fall* (1994), was tame but not domesticated.

Of all the animal species on the planet, humans have managed to domesticate only a few of them. Why? Author and scientist Jared Diamond suggests that it's because an animal can be successfully domesticated only if it meets the following criteria:

1. Flexible diet: The animal can't be too picky. In order for a keeper to keep it alive, the animal must be able to survive on cheap, accessible food sources.

2. Fast growth rate: It must grow quickly enough that

its keeper gets a return on the investment of caring for the animal.

3. Easy to breed: The animals have to procreate easily under the conditions where humans keep them.

4. Easy to get along with: Horses are naturally more gentle than zebras, which have a reputation for being vicious. That's why domestication succeeded with horses but failed with zebras.

5. Doesn't panic: Lots of animals will freak out when they're corralled or restrained. Cows, however, are pretty easygoing, so they were not difficult to domesticate.

6. Adheres to a social hierarchy: Domestication works only if the humans are in charge. Solitary animals like grizzly bears don't go for that. And as far as cats are concerned, it's possible that they domesticated us.

SOME QUESTIONS HAVE NO ANSWERS

"What's the deal with lampshades? If it's a lamp, why do you want shade?"

—JERRY SEINFELD

FASHION

TOGA! TOGA! TOGA!

Q: Did everyone in ancient Rome wear a toga?

A: The modern picture of ancient Rome has everyone wearing long white sheets wrapped around their bodies. That's accurate for the most part, but the Roman Empire lasted more than 1,000 years, and the look and role of the toga changed quite a bit over the centuries. The most widely accepted theory is that togas were created by the Etruscans, Rome's neighbors to the north (until they conquered them around 500 B.C.). The earliest depictions of Romans dressed in togas date back to 753 B.C.

The toga itself was a 20-foot-long sheet made out of wool that was wrapped around the body. It was usually worn over a tunic, basically a long nightshirt that served as underwear. Both men and women wore togas until about 200 B.C.; after that it was only men. (Women wore what's called a *stola*, which was a similar garment made of linen. If a woman was seen in public wearing a toga, she would be labeled a prostitute or an adulterer.)

For the last 600 years of the empire, togas became symbols of the rich and powerful. While they were considered quite fashionable, there was no denying that they weren't very practical, especially during the summer months. They were made of wool, after all. Most Romans stubbornly wore the heavy, cumbersome apparel despite the heat (in public, at least). The discomfort was viewed as an honorable sacrifice for the love of the empire. (Roman soldiers couldn't wear togas; they were much too awkward and cumbersome for battle, so they wore *sagums*, a looser garment that fit well over armor.)

And most togas were white (or off-white), but other colors were used to denote status, or for special occasions. A dark gray or brown *toga pulla* was worn for mourning. The word "candidate" comes from *toga candida*, worn by, you guessed it, political candidates. They were dyed bright white to show how "pure and honest" the politician was. And there were special togas for noblemen, emperors, and even the gods. The fanciest, the *toga picta*, was royal purple. Some Roman slaves were actually trained in "toga construction" so their masters wouldn't have to dress themselves.

SUCH GREAT HEIGHTS

Q: Why did Abraham Lincoln wear a tall top hat?

A: At a towering 6 feet 4 inches, Lincoln quite literally stood head and shoulders above his political opponents. So why would such a tall man want to wear a hat that would make him appear even taller?

According to Debbie Henderson, author of *The Top Hat: An Illustrated History*, towering top hats were considered an "irrepressible symbol of prestige and authority" in the 19th century. While historians can't quite agree on why Lincoln chose to wear various top hats over the years, it was most likely because he felt that they helped him maintain a commanding aura during public appearances.

A more fun theory is that the hat was a gimmick. It helped Lincoln "stand out" from his fellow politicians and make him more memorable, two vital elements to any successful career in public office.

Bonus Fact: In August 1864, a would-be assassin took aim at Lincoln, but the bullet went straight through the hat and missed his head completely. Sadly, on the night that Lincoln was assassinated at Ford's Theatre, he had his hat with him, but it was sitting on the floor next to his seat.

SOME QUESTIONS HAVE NO ANSWERS

"Before birds get sucked into jet engines, do they ever think, 'Is that Rod Stewart in first class?'"

—EDDIE IZZARD

GOING UP

Q: Why do old men wear their pants pulled up so high?

A: There are really only three times in life where your body undergoes a series of rapid changes: as an infant, in adolescence, and when you get really old. Carting around that body for 70-odd years starts to take its toll, and things begin to break down in both expected and unexpected ways. While muscles atrophy and bone density plummets, body fat increases by up to 30 percent. And thanks to some cruel joke, that increase occurs primarily around the midsection.

That happens to be the same spot where aging men have held up their pants for their entire lives. But something has changed: the hips have shrunk, as has the tailbone, but the newly acquired pouch of body fat—and physics—won't allow for the belt to stay up, and the pants start to slip.

There are three options for the aging gentleman: 1) Allow his pants to sag (like those darn kids like to do); 2) wear suspenders (the most adorable option); 3) pull the pants all the way up and over that fatty midsection, which places the belt a few inches below the nipples.

DRESSING DOWN

Q: Why do those darn kids wear their pants so low?

A: Despite the fact many school systems and local governments have banned oversized, low-riding pants, this odd fashion fad is as strong as ever. And it's older than you might think. In the late 1980s, several American penitentiaries banned the wearing of belts. And because standard-issue pants were often too big for inmates, they sagged. Instead of being embarrassed by having to wear clothes that didn't fit, inmates turned it into a fashion statement. The fad spread to the outside world when gang members in Los Angeles started wearing their pants baggy and low in solidarity with their friends in prison. From there, it took off.

The style first found its way into pop culture through rap music. It started with M.C. Hammer's 1990 hit single "U Can't Touch This" and the video, which featured Hammer dancing in oversized "genie" pants. Within a year, the first beltless, boxers-revealing jeans showed up on rap artists such as Ice-T, Too Short, and Kriss Kross (who also ushered in a short-lived craze of wearing the baggy pants backwards).

The trend quickly caught on with teenagers—urban and suburban—and the fashion industry knew it had a winner. By the mid-1990s, brands such as Levi's, J. Crew, Tommy Hilfiger, Savanna, and Khakis had all released "anti-fit" jeans, and within a few years it was a multi-billion dollar industry.

A REAL HEAD-SCRATCHER

Q: Why are hats sized so strangely?

A: A men's sweater can be purchased in small, medium, or large. Shoes are sized in whole and half numbers. Pants (for men) are sized according to the waist size and length. Women's dress sizes are a bit more obtuse, with numbered sizes like 2, 6, and, somehow, 0. So why are hats sized in measurements like "6¾"?

People come in all shapes and sizes, which means clothing needs to run the gamut. But not hats. Despite the wide differences of the body from person to person, nearly all adult heads have a circumference (the distance around it) that falls within the same five-inch span. That's why hat sizes are so specific. But they don't measure actual circumference. It's a number taken from measuring the circumference of a head to the nearest eighth of an inch, and then dividing by pi (3.14159).

It's a little more straightforward in Europe. The hat sizes there are the hat's circumference in centimeters. (Except in France and a few other countries; like the U.S., they have a formula-based system that creates sizes that range from 0 to 9½.)

HERE COMES THE BRIDE

Q: Why do brides wear white dresses?

A: The bride typically wears white to signify purity, either of body or heart, as she enters into a marriage. Whether those things are actually true in every wedding is up for debate, although white remains the color of choice for the bridal dress out of tradition.

Until the 19th century, it was acceptable for brides in Europe and North America to wear wedding dresses in almost any color. Bright colors were favored, because they signified joy. The only colors that were off-limits: black, because it was the color of mourning, and red, because it's what prostitutes wore. (At least in Europe—in many Eastern cultures, red is a symbol of good luck, and it's still the most common wedding dress color in Asia.)

Like many trends and fashions, the idea of a white wedding dress was popularized by royalty. In 1840,

Queen Victoria of England married Prince Albert of Saxe-Coburg and Gotha. She wore a white dress, and the idea took off. A few years later, the major women's magazine of the day, *Godey's Lady's Book*, wrote of wedding dress colors that "white is the most fitting hue, an emblem of purity and innocence."

TIP O' THE CAP

Q: Why do baseball players wear caps?

A: The baseball cap goes all the way back to the 1860s. The Excelsior team of Brooklyn, New York, started wearing caps that consisted of a visor and a button top to keep the sun off their heads and out of their eyes. The hat eventually became known as "Brooklyn-style," and baseball players up and down the eastern seaboard were wearing them by 1900.

Caps proved more practical than fedoras and other types of hats. One advantage: they were less likely to fly off players' heads on windy afternoons at the ballpark. Another advantage: the caps made it easy to display each team's logo on the front over the bill. Within a decade, fans started wearing caps to show their support for their favorite team. Today, the baseball cap has transcended the sport that created it; they're worn by everyone from hip-hop artists to farmers.

GOVERNMENT

FIRST THINGS FIRST

Q: Who was the first First Lady to be called "First Lady"? What were they called before that?

A: From Martha Washington through Julia Grant, presidential wives did not have a title. Martha was called "Lady Washington"; later wives were often called "Mrs. Presidentress."

In 1876, journalist Mary Clemmer Ames referred to Lucy Ware Webb Hayes, wife of the newly elected 19th president, Rutherford B. Hayes, as "the First Lady of the Land" in her column "Woman's Letter from Washington." Lucy Hayes turned out to be a popular First Lady, so the term stuck.

THE POLITICAL DIVIDE

Q: Why are liberals considered "left wing" and conservatives "right wing"?

A: The French Legislative Assembly met for the first time during the French Revolution on October 1, 1791. Like legislative bodies today, this group of 745 lawmakers and representatives grouped themselves according to their political affiliation. For no reason in particular, the more liberal members sat to the left of the speaker, and the conservatives sat to the right. Today, "left wing" and "right wing" are still used to denote those same political viewpoints.

THE WORLD'S MOST FAMOUS TEMP JOB

Q: **How come U.S. legislators and Supreme Court justices can serve indefinitely, but the president only gets two terms?**

A: When the Founding Fathers wrote the original U.S. Constitution in the 1780s, they neglected to include any rules regarding presidential term limits. Nevertheless, George Washington decided to serve as president for only two terms. His gracious act became something of a tradition for his successors (or at least those fortunate enough to get reelected).

During the dark days of the Great Depression and World War II, however, President Franklin Delano Roosevelt was elected to not only a third term but a fourth one as well. He died two years into his final term in 1945. While many Americans lauded Roosevelt's dedication to leading the nation through such a troublesome time, his critics worried about what might happen if a more ruthless president ever attempted to repeat the feat.

Thomas Dewey, Roosevelt's opponent in the 1944 presidential race, was among those who pushed for the 22nd Amendment—which restricts Oval Office occupants to two terms. It was approved by Congress in 1947. After being ratified by enough states by 1951, the amendment was added to the U.S. Constitution.

When it comes to legislators, there are no term

limits, but with Congressional support among Americans at an all-time low, expect to hear a lot about term limits for the House and Senate in the coming years.

A CAPITAL CONUNDRUM

Q: Why is Washington, D.C., referred to as a "district" instead of a state? And where did "Columbia" come from?

A: During its first few decades as a sovereign nation, the United States didn't have an official capital. That meant that members of Congress had to meet in various locations up and down the Eastern Seaboard. So in 1790 Congress passed the Residence Act to establish a permanent location for each of the three federal branches of government.

President George Washington, tasked with finding an ideal location, chose a patch of swampy land on the Potomac River between Virginia and Maryland. This square-shaped land—ten miles on each side—was declared a district instead of a state for various political reasons and in accordance with stipulations outlined in the Constitution. It was also given the name Columbia. At the time, this was a patriotic term for the country that was derived from Christopher Columbus's last name. "District of Columbia" is now usually shortened to "D.C."

With the district established, a spot was chosen for a new city where the three branches would set up shop. The commissioners in charge of the project named the city in honor of President Washington, and Congress met there for the first time in November 1800. These days, both the city and the surrounding district are typically referred to by their collective names: Washington, D.C.

SOME QUESTIONS HAVE NO ANSWERS

"If 95% of accidents happen within the home, where do homeless people go to have 95% of their accidents?"

—STRANGE DE JIM

CLASSLESS COLLEGE

Q: **What exactly is the Electoral College, and how does it pick the president?**

A: In the United States, voters don't directly elect the president. The winner is actually decided by the Electoral College. The "college" is made up of delegates from each state, the number of which is the same as their congressional delegation, plus three for the District of Columbia. For instance, Oklahoma has five representatives and two senators, so it gets seven electoral votes. There are a total of 538 electoral votes, of which 270 are needed to win a presidential election.

Electoral College voters (appointed at the state level

by the two major political parties) are expected to cast their votes according to how their state voted in the general election. And it's a winner-take-all-system: the candidate who received the most popular votes in a state gets all the electoral votes.

The Electoral College usually votes as their constituents have directed, but they don't always. In 2004, a Minnesota elector made a slip-up on his ballot. He accidentally cast his presidential vote for John Edwards, who was the Democratic candidate for vice president, and his vice presidential vote for John Kerry, the candidate for president. (It didn't matter in the end, because Kerry lost to the incumbent George W. Bush.)

WHAT THE HALL?

Q: **Why is a city hall called a "city hall" instead of a "city building"?**

A: Like so many words in the English language, "hall" has multiple meanings. It can refer to a long corridor that leads to one or more rooms, or to a large building. "Hall" is derived from the Old English word *heall*, which once described any large place covered by a roof. It's also connected to the very old Proto-Germanic word *hallo* (which meant the same thing). "Hall" wasn't used as a description for a passageway until sometime in the 17th century. Around the same time, English people also started using it to describe important buildings. British settlers in North America adopted the term and used it for everything from university buildings to manor houses. So that's why the United States is now chock full of city halls, concert halls, convention halls, Halls of Justice, and so on and so forth.

THE BIG SWITCHEROONY

Q: **When did America's two major political parties switch platforms? And why?**

A: The Democrats once ruled the South. Abraham Lincoln, a Republican from the North, ran on an antislavery platform. From then on, Democrats were considered the conservatives, and Republicans were more progressive. What happened?

Political parties switch ideologies more often than you might think. In this case, the Democrats and Republicans remained set in their 19th-century platforms until the late 1920s. Then the Great Depression hit. President Franklin D. Roosevelt, a Democrat, believed the way out of it was via government intervention—more social programs and more safety nets. However, the Republicans held one belief back then that they still hold today: that free-market capitalism—the private sector—is better suited to pull the nation out of economic woes. But it was the practices of Wall Street executives, most of whom were Republicans, that caused the financial collapse that led to the Great Depression. Result: most Americans blamed the hard times on the Republicans, and because of Roosevelt's growing popularity, the power in the executive and legislative branches went mostly to the Democrats—

and stayed with them through World War II.

The Republicans were once again the opposition party, and they needed numbers, so they set their sights on the South, seeking votes by promising a smaller, less intrusive government and, more importantly, states' rights. It was called the "Southern Strategy." The civil rights movement was just getting going, so by catering to the disenfranchised "Dixiecrats" who feared a larger government would take away their freedoms, a shift occurred. By the 1960s, the party started by Abraham Lincoln that had brought about the end of slavery was now the same party that was associated with opposing civil rights.

ALL TALK, NO ACTION

Q: What exactly is a filibuster, and how did it come to be?

A: A filibuster is a legislative tactic usually employed by a member of the minority party to delay a vote that won't go their way. How? By talking…and talking…and talking…for hours on end until everyone has to go home. A recent example: In 2013, Texas state senator Wendy Davis filibustered for 11 hours to try and hold off a vote for increased restrictions on abortion. Per the rules, she could not eat, drink, sit, lean against the podium, or even leave for a bathroom break. (Davis got around those last two rules by wearing a back brace and a urinary catheter.)

The practice of filibustering (but not the word) goes

back to ancient Rome. In 60 B.C., Roman senator Cato the Younger used the tactic to delay a vote to allow Julius Caesar to stand for consul in absentia. Cato talked until nightfall and then invoked a rule that no vote could happen after dusk.

The word itself comes from the Spanish *filibustero*, which means "freebooter" (derived from the Dutch *vrijbuter*). These so-called filibusters took part in illegal expeditions against Cuba, Mexico, and Central America in order to set up local governments that would apply to the United States for annexation. The word entered the political arena in 1853 when Representative Albert G. Brown (D-MS) complained about a fellow politician's "filibustering intervention" in Cuba.

A TANGLED WEB

Q: Did Al Gore really claim that he invented the Internet? And did he?

A: In March 1999, Vice President Al Gore was preparing for a run at the White House. During an interview with Wolf Blitzer on CNN, he was asked why Democrats should vote for him in the primaries instead of Senator Bill Bradley. That's when Gore made the statement that would haunt him for years to come.

His exact quote: "During my service in the United States Congress, I took the initiative in creating the Internet." So he didn't quite claim that he *invented* the Internet, but his awkward phrasing created a punchline that's still used against him two decades later.

But Gore did play a vital part in expanding the Internet. When he was a U.S. senator, he was the primary sponsor of the 1991 High-Performance Computing and Communications Act, so much so that it became known as "the Gore Bill."

Gore spent two years fighting to get the bill pushed through Congress (while also popularizing the term "information superhighway"). Result: the bill passed. A portion of the $600 million in federal funding went to developers of various computer systems to create Mosaic, a web browser that eventually paved the way for Netscape, Yahoo, and eventually Google.

For what it's worth, Gore was inducted into the Internet Hall of Fame in 2012 for his contribution. As the organization's website puts it: "Instrumental in helping to create the 'Information Superhighway,' Gore was one of the first government officials to recognize that the Internet's impact could reach beyond academia to fuel educational and economic growth as well."

TECHNOLOGY

FUTURE IMPERFECT

Q: Where the heck is my flying car?

A: Calm yourself, McFly. The technology is already here. The first flying car prototypes were built back in the 1920s, and automakers have been tinkering with designs ever since…to varying degrees of success. The actual reason the skies aren't filled with flying cars has more to do with economics, politics, and public safety than technology.

First off, a flying car wouldn't necessarily be a car that can fly in the air, but a plane that can drive on the ground. They would be larger—and way more expensive—than most cars, and integrating them into our existing infrastructure would be a monumental task. For more than a century, we've been using a system of roadways that does a really good job of getting people where they need to go. Automobile technology has steadily improved to the point where we drive smaller, faster, safer cars that can drive quite close to each other on crowded roads and highways. Adding flying cars would require an entire redesign of the world's roads and parking lots (would they be renamed "landing lots"?).

And perhaps the biggest detriment: flying cars would be more dangerous than cars. You may have heard that air travel is the safest way to travel. That's because pilots spend years training for their licenses. Imagine that rowdy neighbor of yours (the one with all the junk in his yard) getting drunk and taking his flying car out for a joyride. Even scarier: nefarious types (thieves, terrorists, etc.) could use flying cars to land in secured areas.

The logistics alone would be too much for the Federal Aviation Administration, which regulates air travel, to handle. And most police forces are overtaxed as it is. Flying cars would require a completely new government agency, which is a nonstarter in today's volatile political climate.

So the next big change in personal travel won't be taking to the air, it will be switching to more energy-efficient, driverless cars and high-speed public transportation.

All that being said, there are a few companies out there trying to perfect a flying car. In the early 2010s, Massachusetts-based automaker Terrafugia (Latin for "escape the earth") started work on the TF-X, touting it as the world's first fully autonomous flying car. With a flight range of 500 miles and a cruising speed of around 200 mph, the designers hope to have it available for mass production in the 2020s. Other flying cars in various stages of development include the Xplorair, a vehicle being designed in France, and the SkyRider X2R, which yielded an operable 1:5 scale prototype in 2015. But for the foreseeable future, flying cars will only be novelty toys for the rich.

MIXED SIGNALS

Q: **Can your cell phone really crash an airplane?**

A: "Please turn off all portable electronic devices." This ubiquitous announcement comes over the cabin loudspeakers twice—when an airplane is taxiing toward a runway, and right before it lands. Is this rule there just to annoy you? Or is there really a possibility that a smartphone or an e-reader could interfere with the navigation system and other equipment on board?

In 2003, a chartered plane in New Zealand crashed while attempting to land at an airport in Christchurch. News reports claimed that the pilot accidentally left his cell phone on, and that must have caused the accident. An investigation concluded that the crash—one of the worst in New Zealand's history—was not caused by a cell phone, but by a pilot who was dangerously incompetent. (He was using a GPS unit instead of the plane's instruments.) Nevertheless, the incident is often cited as a reason why passengers are required to keep their electronic devices turned off during takeoffs and landings.

Updated technology and aviation equipment has all but eliminated the risks on newer aircraft, but older commercial planes don't have them. So what would happen if every passenger on your next flight decided to play Angry Birds on their phones during takeoff? Probably nothing, but as the old saying goes: "Better safe than sorry."

And finally, there is a practical reason for this rule: because most plane crashes occur during landing and takeoff, it's important during these times that passengers' attention isn't divided between the announcements from the flight deck and their Facebook feed.

WRITING WITH A ROCK

Q: Is there really lead in a pencil?

A: Thankfully, no. That notion goes all the way back to the ancient Greeks, Romans, and Egyptians, who used small lead disks for drawing guidelines on papyrus before writing above them with brushes and ink. Centuries later, artists in Europe used metallic rods of lead, silver, and zinc to make very light drawings.

But that all changed in 1564 when a graphite deposit was unearthed in Borrowdlae, England. Using graphite for writing wasn't new; the Aztecs did it long before the arrival of Columbus. But it was new to the Europeans. They discovered that the soft graphite—a form of carbon—made rich, dark lines. They began carving pointed "marking stones" out of it and using the stones to write with. One problem: the stones marked up the writer's hands as much as the paper. Eventually, people figured out that they could wrap a string around the writing stick to keep their hands clean, unwinding the string as the graphite wore down. That was the first version of the modern pencil.

INTO THE WOODS

Q: How do they get the graphite into the pencil?

A: A better way to phrase that question might be: How do they get the wood around the graphite? First, the graphite is ground up and mixed with fine clay. The more clay that's added, the harder the "lead." Then the mixture is forced through an "extruder" to make a long, thin rod. The rod is fired at a temperature of 1,832°F to harden it and then treated with wax for smooth writing.

Meanwhile, the wood is sawed into small boards—each the length of one pencil, with the width of seven pencils, and the thickness of half a pencil. Seven tiny grooves are cut lengthwise. Then the lead is laid into each of them, and an identical board is glued on top. A machine cuts the boards into nine individual pencils. Last step: they're coated with nontoxic paint. Now, the completed pencil is ready to write up to 45,000 words.

GETTING AROUND

Q: Why are manhole covers round?

A: If the heavy iron covers were any other shape—square, rectangle, oval, etc.—then if they were turned to a certain angle, they could fall through the hole. By making them round, no matter how hard you try, there is no way to get one to fall through.

SPACE SUDS

Q: How exactly does an astronaut get clean?

A: The International Space Station has a shower, something the space shuttle astronauts had to live without.

(They had to make do with sponge baths and shampoo, originally designed for hospital patients, that didn't need to be rinsed out.)

Taking a shower in space is similar to taking one on Earth, except that in the absence of gravity, the water doesn't fall to the floor. It just floats around inside the shower stall, which is sealed to prevent the water from escaping into the rest of the station. One advantage: because the water floats around instead of going down the drain, you don't need as much to take your shower as you would on Earth. You only use about a gallon of water, and instead of moving in and out from under the showerhead, you just grab the floating globs of water and rub them on yourself. When you're finished, pull the vacuum hose from the wall and suck up all the drops. Then you can get back to doing space stuff.

NOT AS CLUMSY OR RANDOM AS A BLASTER

Q: Could lightsabers work in the real world?

A: *Star Wars* is more space fantasy than science fiction, so creator George Lucas didn't put a lot of thought into how his laser swords actually worked. But that hasn't stopped actual scientists from studying various forms of light and how it could possibly be used to alter solid objects.

In 2013, a team of researchers from MIT and Harvard University revealed that they'd found a way to bind photons together in order to create new light molecules that could, conceivably, bond together to form a glowing blade. Sadly, that's not the scientists' ultimate goal; they're more interested in using the photons to design a supercomputer. Nevertheless, their findings could one day be used to create, as Obi-Wan Kenobi put it, "an elegant weapon for a more civilized age."

Meanwhile, physicists at the University of Queensland in Australia have been performing similar experiments. As researcher Martin Ringbauer said in 2015, the biggest problem that his team had encountered was figuring out how to get the lightsaber blade to halt at a designated point: "You can't just make a laser stop without it hitting something solid or being reflected back on itself with a mirror." So if they ever do manage to build a lightsaber, its blade will stretch far, far away.

#SMALL_TALK

Q: Why are Twitter posts limited to 140 characters?

A: This limit comes from text messaging. One of the architects of that form of communication was a German communications researcher named Friedhelm Hillebrand, who served as chairman of the non-voice services committee for the Global System for Mobile Communications. In 1985, he typed out a bunch of what he thought would be typical text messages and noticed that none of them went over 160 characters, so he set that as the limit for phone texting. When mobile phone companies later began to add text messaging to their plans, they went with the 160-character limit.

And then when Twitter was launched in 2006, it was designed to be primarily used on mobile phones. So CEO Jack Dorsey adopted the 160-character limit, but he took off 20 characters to make room for the users' addresses, which left the number at 140.

In 2016, Twitter made big news when several media outlets reported that the social media giant would expand its message size to 10,000 characters. But the rumors were quashed when Dorsey said, "It's staying. It's a good constraint for us and it allows for of-the-moment brevity."

Bonus Fact: Why is it called Twitter? Because its original code name was "twttr" (inspired by similar code name–inspired websites like Flickr). Dorsey recalled, "We came across the word 'twitter,' and it was just perfect. The definition was 'a short burst of incon-sequential information,' and 'chirps from birds.' And that's exactly what the product was."

PIXELATED PREDICAMENT

Q: **How come video games never look as good as they do in commercials?**

A: The gaming industry has come a long way over the past 25 years, when 16-bit graphics were still the standard for home gaming consoles. Back in those days, Nintendo and Sega grappled over which of their systems, the Super Nintendo or the Sega Genesis, offered superior visuals with their 2-D graphics.

The industry became even more competitive in the late 1990s when the Sony PlayStation upped the ante with more elaborate gameplay and 3-D environments. But there were lots of growing pains. For example, the first *Tomb Raider* game, released in 1996, looked dreadful by today's standards.

To distract gamers from clunky visuals in advertisements, the companies would simply hide them. One famous example involved a series of TV commercials for *Final Fantasy VII*, the PlayStation's biggest release of 1997. Instead of focusing on the game's uninviting graphics, the ads showed only its far more detailed "cutscenes" (cinematic sequences that feature more sophisticated animation). Then, when gamers played at home, they discovered the actual in-game graphics looked nothing like the commercials.

Despite a slew of complaints, the trend continues to this day; most of the industry's TV ads are crammed with cutscenes instead of gameplay. That way, they look a lot more fun to play. A 2016 commercial for *Batman: Arkham Knight* consists almost entirely of cutscene imagery. If you look closely at this and other, similar ads, whenever the graphics get clunky, you can see tiny words pop up on the bottom of the screen that say "actual game play." For this reason, most stores will let you play a game before buying it.

MYTHS &
LEGENDS

BOO!

Q: **Why are ghosts depicted as a white sheet?**

A: The origin of this odd custom is unclear. The most likely theory is that it comes from stage plays in western Europe. Up until the 19th century or so, not everyone who died was buried in a coffin. A wooden box was expensive. Most poor people were placed directly into the ground wrapped in a white burial shroud, essentially an oversized white sheet. If a character appeared on stage in one of these sheets, the audience would instantly recognize it as a ghost.

OCEAN FARTS

Q: **Why have so many ships and planes gone missing in the Bermuda Triangle?**

A: Located in the Atlantic Ocean between the tip of Florida and the islands of Puerto Rico and Bermuda, the 500,000-square-mile Bermuda Triangle has been blamed for dozens of mysterious disappearances over the years. Entire squadrons of warplanes have vanished without a trace. Ships have shown up to port without anyone on board. A luxury liner went down in 1918 without even sending a distress signal. What's the cause? Space aliens? Interdimensional portals? Time travel?

First and foremost, the Bermuda Triangle is one of the most heavily trafficked areas in the world, so it's no surprise that there have been a lot of shipwrecks and plane crashes in the region—which is also known for nasty weather. Because of all the lore surrounding the Bermuda Triangle, many of these incidents are given an added meaning simply because they happened there.

But the most fascinating theory has to do with the planet's geothermal activity. Methane pockets on the seafloor have been known to emit gas eruptions that rise swiftly up to the surface and even into the air. A passing ship or plane that finds itself in the path of one of these eruptions would have no time to react. This phenomenon, though scientifically sound, has never been observed. So for now, it remains a theory. But it's more likely than time-traveling aliens…or is it?

YOU'RE BEING WATCHED

Q: Why do the eyes in a painting or photograph seem to follow you?

A: The picture isn't haunted. This odd optical illusion occurs because the subject was looking directly at the painter, or the camera, when the portrait was made. The reason this happens is that the picture is not three-dimensional, like a sculpture or a living person. Because there are only two dimensions, no matter where you are when you look at it, you're only ever seeing a flat surface. So the subject will always be looking at you. The opposite is also true: if the subject was looking off to the side, then no matter where you view the picture from, the subject will never, ever look at you. (If it does, run.)

TRICK OR...TURKEY?

Q: Why do kids dress up in costumes and go trick-or-treating on Halloween?

A: As weird as it might sound, this beloved Halloween tradition was once a Thanksgiving tradition. In the early 19th century, poor people in the northeastern U.S. were known to go from door to door the night before Thanksgiving to ask for something to eat. Children started dressing up in raggedy clothing and imitating these unfortunate souls as a practical joke.

The idea of dressing up (or, in this case, dressing "down") became synonymous with Thanksgiving, so much so that when Abraham Lincoln declared it an official national holiday in 1863, people celebrated with masquerade balls instead of turkey and stuffing. Toward the end of the 19th century, Thanksgiving parades caught on, which further encouraged people to run around in costumes.

Children, mostly in East Coast cities, celebrated the holiday by dressing up as clowns or hoboes and knocking on neighborhood doors to ask for free treats. It became so common that Thanksgiving got the nickname "Ragamuffin Day" in many communities.

But not everyone liked the idea of costumed kids begging them for food, especially during the Great Depression, when food was scarce. The practice slowly died out, and Thanksgiving became a more low-key holiday to celebrate family (but the parades remained).

Some grumpy grown-ups took it a step further, and

heated up pennies until they were red-hot, and then offered them as tricks. Gradually, tricks and treats became intertwined.

Halloween, meanwhile, had been in America since the 1840s, but it was mostly reserved for adults. In the 1930s, American kids took the old Thanksgiving tradition and applied it to Halloween. The first known mention of trick-or-treating comes from a November 1, 1934, article in the *Oregon Journal* called "Halloween Pranks Keep Police on Hop": "Other young goblins and ghosts, employing modern shakedown methods, successfully worked the 'trick or treat' system in all parts of the city."

RUNNING OUT

Q: Why are horseshoes considered lucky?

A: This superstition has crossed many cultures. Pagans thought horseshoes were lucky because they were made of iron, a sacred metal of great power. The Norse god of war, Thor, wielded an iron hammer.

The ancient Greeks thought the horseshoe had a lucky shape because it resembled a new moon, a sign of fertility. That shape was considered lucky in the Middle Ages, too. Medieval church doors were sometimes shaped like a crescent moon.

But it was the tenth-century legend of a blacksmith named Dunstan that sealed the lucky fate of horseshoes. When a man came in asking to be shod in horseshoes, Dunstan realized that the request was unusual. Then he saw that his customer had a cloven foot—he was shoeing the devil himself! Dunstan, who later became archbishop of Canterbury, tortured the devil with hot irons and nails until the devil promised that neither he nor any of his demons would enter a building protected by a horseshoe. The horseshoe must be nailed onto the building facing upward so that its luck doesn't run out.

FEETS OF FANCY

Q: Why are rabbits' feet considered lucky?

A: Rabbits and their wild cousin, the hare, have been associated since pagan times with spring, renewal, and fertility. (That's how we got the Easter Bunny.) In the Middle Ages, hares were associated with witches, who were said to be able to change themselves into rabbits. Despite elements of witchery, the hare was still considered a lucky animal because of its many offspring and its burrowing habits. Fearing what lay buried under the earth, people admired the rabbit's ability to live underground and still survive.

Eventually, the legends surrounding hares and rabbits—legends of fertility, the ability to survive evil, and magical powers—became associated with the "luck" in the left hind foot of a rabbit. Though not for the rabbit, of course.

AS YOU WISH

Q: Was *The Princess Bride* based on a real legend?

A: Sadly, no. The 1987 movie is based on a 1973 novel by William Goldman. But Goldman's book, as stated in the introduction, is an abridged version of a 200-year-old folk tale that he took from a much longer book of the same name by a reclusive writer named S. Morgenstern. *The Princess Bride* is, in fact, one of the most beloved stories of Morgenstern's home country of Florin (where the book takes place).

There's no such place as Florin, and no such writer as S. Morgenstern. Goldman wrote the book, and the idea that he abridged it from an older novel was used as a literary device.

ATTACK OF THE CLOWNS

Q: Why are so many people afraid of clowns?

A: The fear of clowns is called *coulrophobia*. Although very few people have ever been officially diagnosed with the condition, if you post a clown pic onto Facebook, you'd think that 90 percent of the population thinks they're evil…or at least creepy. It relates to a phenomenon that psychologist Sigmund Freud called "the Uncanny." This is a juxtaposition that results when a recognizable image is heavily distorted or disfigured, but still recognizable in its original form. In this case, a smiling face, which people usually find pleasing, is made "uncanny" by adding makeup, a big red nose, and a big red perma-grin that won't go away no matter how sad the clown is inside. Although the makeup is meant to create an aura of happiness and fun—especially for kids—the concept of permanent happiness can come across as unnatural. Furthermore, it hides the clown's humanity, which the subconscious brain interprets as a sign of untrustworthiness.

According to the University at Buffalo's Andrew Stott, an English professor who specializes in clowns (someone has to), this cultural distrust can be traced back to medieval times, when jesters were often associated with death and corruption. "Clowns have always been associated with danger and fear," Stott explains, "because they push logic up to its breaking point. They push our understanding to the limits of reason and they do this through joking but also through ridicule."

Real clowns, whose mission is to bring joy to children of all ages, hate this stereotype. Sadly, their reputation has not been helped by some truly scary clowns, both real and fictional. There's the murderous clown Pennywise from the Stephen King horror novel *It*. The Insane Clown Posse, a hip-hop duo, features two "wicked clowns" named Violent J and Shaggy 2 Dope.

And in real life, there's the French clown Jean-Gaspard Deburau, who in 1836 killed a child that was teasing him. And the worst clown of all: John Wayne Gacy, who was executed for the murder of 33 men in the 1970s. Press reports never failed to mention that, in between murders, he worked as a children's party clown named Pogo.

SCIENCE

WHAT A NICE DAY!

Q: Why is the sky blue?

A: The light that comes from the Sun contains multiple colors, but it appears white to us. When that light hits Earth's atmosphere, the colors are sent scattering (kind of like a water balloon after it hits a wall) because they bounce off all of the particles and gases in the atmosphere. Because blue light travels in shorter and smaller waves then the other colors, it gets scattered across a wider area. This causes it to blot out the other colors in the spectrum, so the sky appears blue instead of violet, green, etc. This same process also impacts sunsets. When the sun appears low on the horizon, the blue light is scattered across an even wider area. This allows yellow and red to light up the horizon in its place.

IT'S A BIRD! IT'S A PLANE! IT'S...A CLOUD?

Q: Why do clouds float?

A: Clouds are comprised of millions of tiny water droplets that would all plummet to Earth immediately if not for two factors: wind currents and friction. Each drop is very, very light, and its surface area is large in comparison to its weight. As a result, wind currents have more effect upon the droplets than gravity does, so they fly around inside the cloud (much like an electrical fan that blows a feather across a room).

All of this blowing around creates friction, which causes water droplets to bump into each other and cling together. Once they grow large enough, their weight overpowers the friction and wind, so—depending on the temperature—they fall to the ground in the form of rain, sleet, hail, snow, etc.

SOME QUESTIONS HAVE NO ANSWERS

"At what age is it appropriate to tell a highway it's adopted?"

—ZACH GALIFIANAKIS

DON'T BE SO DENSE

Q: **If heat rises, why is it so much colder at high altitudes?**

A: Heat doesn't really rise. When air comes into contact with warm ground, it acquires some of that heat and grows less dense, so it rises (as lighter things tend to do). As the air rises, it mixes with cooler air, cooling it to a point where it's too dense to rise any more. Because the cool air on a mountaintop (or high in the sky) doesn't make contact with the warmer ground, it remains cold.

SLOWSAND

Q: Why is it called "quicksand" when you sink very, very slowly?

A: Most of our knowledge of quicksand comes from old movies and cartoons, but it doesn't really work like that in real life. First of all, quicksand isn't really sand but rather a gel that's created when sand mixes with water where there's no natural outlet, so it has nowhere to go but to soak into the sand. This forms a suspension where the sand doesn't dissolve but is dispersed through the water, making it a spongy semisolid. The suspension is broken when the surface tension is disrupted, like when you inadvertently walk into it. That makes the quicksand separate into water and compacted, wet sediment.

If you do find yourself sinking into quicksand, relax. Don't bother struggling; you aren't going to get sucked below the surface, because quicksand pits are only a few feet deep. But they do create a powerful suction effect, enough to suck off a boot. And if you become exhausted trying to free yourself, you could fall over and potentially drown. Instead, slowly lean until you're "floating" on your back, and slowly spread out your arms and legs. The quicksand is so dense that it will push your body to the surface, at which point you can slowly shimmy your way back to solid ground (a lot filthier than when you went in there).

As for the name, the "quick" doesn't refer to the rate at which a person sinks in it. It's a derivative of the old

English expression "stuck quick," which means "stuck permanently."

HUNGRY PLANET

Q: **Can sinkholes form anywhere? Could one form underneath you right now?**

A: A sinkhole is simply a hole in the ground, created through naturally occurring water drainage and/or soil erosion. That escaping water can make a hole just a few feet wide, or it could grow into a monster that will swallow an entire city block. Therein lies the difference between the two types of sinkholes, and why they don't usually occur spontaneously. Both kinds of sinkholes occur in *karst* terrain. These are areas where bedrock (limestone or gypsum) gets dissolved by water. Here's how they differ.

• A *cover-subsidence sinkhole* forms (or emerges) over many years or even decades. With this "long-term sinkhole," erosion causes the soil at ground level to dissipate and expose the bedrock underneath. Water slowly seeps in and wears down the rock, creating holes that fill with water, which then escapes and leaves a hole in its absence.

• A *cover-collapse sinkhole*, however, can and does appear relatively suddenly—or at least it seems sponta- neous because its warning signs have been obscured. The cracks and openings caused by water erosion happen far below the surface. Water drains out, but soil and sediment remain perched precariously on top of the eroding ground until…it doesn't anymore. Once the ground cover sinks under its own weight, it collapses to reveal a sinkhole that has been forming for who knows how long.

There is a chance a sinkhole could form underneath you right now, so long as you live in an area with a lot of natural limestone and gypsum bedrock, coupled with unseasonal heavy rainfall that the ground isn't used to absorbing.

CARBON (NOT) COPIES

Q: If diamonds and graphite are both made of carbon, why are they so different?

A: You probably know that diamonds and graphite (most commonly seen as "lead" in pencils) are made of exactly the same stuff—the chemical element carbon. But diamonds are among the hardest substances known, and graphite is very soft. Why so different? Because the atoms that make up each one are bonded in different configurations due to factors such as pressure, temperature, and neighboring elements.

Diamonds are the result of a lot of pressure; graphite, not so much. This is known as *allotropy* (from the Greek *allos*, "other," and *tropos*, "manner"), and the varying substances that result from these atomic arrangements are known as "allotropes of an element." This only relates to substances that are composed of just one element. (There are no allotropes of water, for example, which is composed of two elements: hydrogen and oxygen.)

Allotropy occurs in several elements—including oxygen, nitrogen, and phosphorus, but the most common examples are the allotropes of carbon.

The carbon atoms in diamonds are bonded in a three-dimensional lattice configuration. Each atom is very strongly bonded to four other atoms in four different directions—on different planes. This results in all the atoms having a perfectly symmetrical, interlocking pattern throughout a given stone. That arrangement is what gives diamonds their particular physical characteristics—how they react to light, their distinctive hardness, and their resistance to electric current.

Each atom in a piece of graphite is bonded to three other atoms in three different directions, but, unlike diamonds, all on the same plane. They form sheets of carbon, each just one atom thick. Those sheets are bonded to each other, but only very weakly, so they're able to slip and slide over each other and easily come apart—like a deck of playing cards. This is what makes graphite so soft and "slippery," and is why it's used in pencils, where some of it easily slides off onto paper. (It's also used industrially as a "dry lubricant.")

THE AQUAMAN PARADOX

Q: **We need oxygen to breathe, and there is oxygen in water. So how come we can drown in water?**

A: It's because the oxygen atoms are in two different states. The oxygen floating around in the atmosphere is in what's called a free state, meaning you can inhale them freely into your lungs.

But when it comes to water, each oxygen atom is chemically bonded to two hydrogen atoms (which is why we call it H_2O). That chemical bond is so strong that the atoms can only be separated by sending an electrical current through the water in such a way that they will revert to their free states. That process is called *electrolysis*. And because your body can't do this, the oxygen atoms in water will do your lungs no good at all.

HUES WHO?

Q: Why are lakes different colors?

A: It all has to do with which substances are suspended in the water. Sediments cause brown water, and algae usually make it green. Tannic acids leached from leaves can make water look black. Minerals, like the reddish-brown tint from iron, can make a lake look red. And some lakes are bluer than the sky. Here's a rundown:

• Deep blue: Crater Lake in Oregon gets its deep blue color because its water is so pure and deep. (In fact, it's the deepest lake in the United States, with a maximum depth of 1,946 feet.) Sunlight penetrates very deep into the clear water, and the depth absorbs the sun's longer rays, like red and yellow. It also reflects the shortest rays...like blue and violet. So on sunny days the lake is dark blue.

• Turquoise: Peyto Lake in Canada is glacier-fed. Nearby glaciers erode the bedrock, grinding it up into bits of rock and sediment called glacier flour. The flour then tumbles into the lake, where it makes the waters turquoise.

• Pink: The nearly dry Owens Lake in California gets its rosy pink color from the millions of halobacteria that feed on its shallow, salty brine. These bacteria carry a pigment that turns them pink or red.

• Multicolored: The three Kelimutu Lakes in Indonesia each filled up a separate crater of the same volcano… and they change color. Sometimes one lake will be blue while another is green and another is red or brown. Then they swap. The lakes' colors are triggered by changing minerals and acids from volcanic activity.

MOTION IN THE OCEAN

Q: Why don't oceans freeze in winter?

A: One reason is that they're always moving. The oceans contain huge amounts of water that are in constant motion—they rarely ever sit still long enough to freeze. Plus, water from warmer oceans is always flowing into the colder ones and changing the temperatures. Another reason is that the oceans are full of salt, which has a lower freezing point than water.

There are two exceptions, however. At the North and South Poles, the ocean does freeze. The surface of the

Arctic Ocean at the North Pole, for instance, freezes 10 to 15 feet down, insulating the water beneath it and keeping it from freezing completely.

THROUGH THE HAZE

Q: Why do stars appear to twinkle?

A: Despite what the old English lullaby would have you believe, stars neither twinkle, nor are they little. Because they're so far away, they look small to our eyes. (Okay, maybe that part's obvious.)

　　By the time the light from those distant suns reaches our eyes, it had to travel thousands of light-years through space. That didn't affect how we see it too much (unless the light passed through a nebula), but when the light hits Earth's atmosphere, it has to travel through gases, dust, salt, water vapor, and other ingredients. That's why stars appear to twinkle; we're viewing it through a very dirty lens.

SHOOTING BLANKS

Q: What exactly are shooting stars, and why aren't they more dangerous?

A: It sounds like a nightmare scenario: a space rock crashes into our atmosphere at breakneck speed and erupts into a massive fireball that lights up the sky as it hurls toward the ground with incredible force! Everybody run! The sky is falling!

No, it isn't.

Millions of these space rocks enter our atmosphere every year, and so far, only seven of them have been known to hit someone. That's in all of recorded history. So why aren't humans being picked off like flies?

Because these so-called shooting stars are actually meteors, and their bark is much bigger than their bite. They usually come from comets (especially true when they're a part of a meteor shower). When a comet passes near the Sun, it leaves particles of rock and dust in its wake, called *meteoroids*. When Earth passes near or through this trail of comet debris, some of the meteoroids are pulled in by gravity and then pass into our atmosphere—which quickly slows them down. (It's not unlike throwing a small rock into a pond.) We see a streak of light in the night sky, caused by vaporization of the meteoroid's particles. That's when the meteoroid becomes a meteor, or shooting star.

Most meteors are no larger than the toenail on your little toe. Many are just the size of a grain of sand. But some can be the size of your fist and, in rare cases, the size of a large dog or even a car. Most burn out before reaching the ground, but when a large meteor enters the atmosphere, it can survive the descent.

Most of the meteors disappear into the water (which covers most of the planet), never to be seen again. But some are found on land—especially on the Antarctic icefields. (If a rock is found there, it can only be from a meteor, since there are no other rocks around.) When a meteor lands on the surface of the Earth, it becomes a *meteorite*. They're hard to find because, to the untrained eye, they look just like any other rock.

LIFE IN THE FAST LANE

Q: How fast are you traveling right now?

A: "I'm not traveling right now," you may be thinking. "I'm sitting here reading this book!" Well, even though *you* may be sitting still, planet Earth sure isn't. It's kind of like riding in a car; your body may not be moving, but it is certainly in motion. In fact, in the time it takes you to read this sentence, you'll have traveled thousands of miles. Take a deep breath…and you've traveled thousands more!

Our planet is spinning at 1,040 miles per hour at the equator. At the same time, it's traveling around the Sun at 67,000 mph. And our Sun is moving through our local star cluster at 45,000 mph. Our local star cluster rides on the outer spiral arm of our galaxy, which is rotating at another 515,000 mph. Our galaxy is moving through what we call the Local Group of galaxies at about 180,000 mph. And the Local Group is moving through the universe at an estimated 540,000 mph. Added up, that's…really fast!

FOOD & DRINK

A COUPLE OF FLAKES

Q: Why do we put milk on cereal?

A: Starting the day with a bowl of cold grains and milk is a relatively new phenomenon. Up until the late 1800s, meat was what's for breakfast: usually eggs, ham, sausage, bacon, or cheap steaks. German immigrants to the U.S. brought the breakfast meat tradition with them. Other cultures had their own breakfast traditions: the Scots and Irish brought oatmeal, the Russians introduced porridge (called *kasha*) made of barley, and in the South, corn grits were (and still are) part of the most important meal of the day. Other European immigrants brought along muesli, a mix of grains, fruits, and nuts, but it didn't catch on in the U.S. the way bacon, porridge, and oatmeal did.

That changed in the 1890s when the Kellogg brothers, John and Will, opened the Battle Creek Sanitarium in Michigan. Health food advocates as well as Seventh-day Adventists, the Kelloggs didn't eat meat, and they spread the idea to visitors. They believed fiber was the key to health, and served dried flakes made of mashed and toasted corn. They called this concoction Corn Flakes. It caught on so well that we still eat it today, and it has the same basic recipe.

The lack of meat in the diet left a protein deficiency, which the Kelloggs recommended be alleviated by pouring protein-rich milk over dry cereal. It also made the flakes more palatable, as well as logical—milk was commonly added to porridge and oatmeal.

When the Kelloggs started marketing their new cereals, their ads had to explain the concept to customers: boxes of Corn Flakes were pictured next to bottles of milk, a helpful serving suggestion.

Bonus Fact: Ironically, the Kellogg brothers were staunch vegetarians, but their name comes from a medieval English surname for a butcher; it literally meant "kill hog."

POOR LITTLE GUY

Q: Why are live lobsters placed into boiling water?

A: It's for your own good to boil a lobster alive—otherwise you could get really sick or even die. Lobsters and many other shellfish harbor loads of toxic bacteria in their flesh. The bacteria don't harm the living lobster, but once it kicks the bucket, the bacteria try to take over, so they amp up production, rapidly releasing toxins into the otherwise delicious lobster meat. The only solution: kill the bacteria immediately. Cooking the lobster alive doesn't give bacteria a chance to reproduce. The one loser in this whole situation is the lobster. Which leads us to our next question.

IN HOT WATER

Q: Do lobsters feel pain?

A: The jury is still out on what lobsters actually "feel" when they're being boiled alive. It certainly looks like they're not enjoying themselves—their muscles twitch and they sometimes emit a high-pitched whine that sounds to some like they're screaming in agony. The good news: that scream is just steam escaping, and the twitching is involuntary. The bad news: lobsters might still feel pain. Some studies maintain that they do, while others say the opposite, maintaining that crustaceans are just large insects with primitive brains that don't necessarily interpret the burning as pain. That's the official conclusion of the Lobster Institute of Maine, whose experts maintain that "cooking a lobster is like cooking a big bug." Their primitive brains don't interpret pain like we do.

Pain or not, watching a live lobster get boiled can be unsettling for a lot of people—after all, there isn't really any other recipe that begins with "kill the animal first"—so the institute has released guidelines for preparing the lobster in such a way that "minimizes our own trauma."

The easiest way (short of buying a really expensive zapper) is to place the lobster in cold water first, or in the fridge for a while—while being careful not freeze it. This will slow the lobster's system down so it's barely conscious when you put it in the pot. Some chefs like to utilize the "quick-kill technique" of inserting a knife point into the back of the lobster's head, an inch below the eyes, in the middle of the back—and then immediately put it into the boiling water.

1

TIME TO MILK THE STEAK

Q: **Why are there different names for live animals and their meat?**

A: Beef comes from cows. Pork comes from pigs. Mutton comes from sheep. It's certainly an odd linguistic practice that we use one word to refer to an animal when it's alive and others for when it becomes food.

This quirk goes all the way back to the birth of "modern" England: the Norman conquest of 1066. Duke William II of Normandy, later known as William the Conqueror, led troops from Normandy, Breton, and France to seize control of the British crown, to which he held claim. Essentially French, these groups became the ruling class in England. The previous tenants of England, the Anglo-Saxons, were suddenly second-class citizens, and as such they were relegated to menial jobs, particularly the tending of farm animals.

But the peasant Anglo-Saxons didn't get to eat much of those animals' meat—the ruling Normans did. They had their own names for animals because they spoke Norman, a precursor to modern French. So the Anglo-Saxon farmers who tended to the live animals called them by their Old English names, and the Normans, who didn't farm them but ate them, continued to call them by their Norman names.

A few examples: the Old English word for "cow" was *cū*, and the Normans called it *buef* (from which English got "cow" and "beef"). The Anglo-Saxons called pigs *swin* or *picga* ("swine" and "pig"), and the Normans called it *porc* (which became pork). Hens to the Anglo-Saxons: *henn* (hen) or *cicen* (chicken). To the Normans: *pouletrie* (poultry).

EYES WIDE SHUT

Q: How many cups of coffee would you have to drink in order to kill yourself?

A: Without the aid of coffee, this book would have never made it to press on time. But how much coffee is too much? The first thing to keep in mind is that caffeine is a drug, and as it is with any drug, no matter how beneficial or harmless, it is possible to overdose and even die from consuming too much of it.

And that's been a real problem in the 21st century thanks to powdered caffeine and caffeinated diet pills. (In 2006, a teenager in Connecticut died after downing 24 No-Doz tablets.) According to the U.S. Food and Drug Administration, the average adult can safely consume about 400 milligrams of caffeine per day. Depending on body weight, studies suggest that roughly ten times that amount would cause an adult to overdose, but tolerance can also play a factor, as does how quickly it's ingested.

Downing too many caffeine pills is more likely to lead to an overdose simply because it's a lot more difficult to drink that same amount of caffeine in coffee form. A 16-ounce cup of brewed coffee from Starbucks contains about 330 milligrams of caffeine. Using this as an example, if you're an adult, you'd need to drink 12 cups fairly quickly just to achieve an overdose, a nearly impossible task. That's over a gallon of coffee, and your stomach would start fighting you at a certain point. So you'd probably vomit it all up before it killed you.

PARTS IS PARTS

Q: **What's really in a hot dog?**

A: After meat processors cut off the steaks and hams and other expensive bits from the animals, all of the "trimmings" left over are ground up into a cheap sausage. Behold: the hot dog.

Before you throw up in your mouth a bit, it's not as bad as you've heard; your ballpark frank isn't necessarily "cow anuses and pig guts." Okay, there might be a wee bit of those things, but hot dogs are primarily made out of gristle, fat, fatty tissue, and offal, including head meat, feet, skin, blood, and the liver. All those trimmings are ground up together in an industrial machine, extruded through a metal sieve, and blended until it forms a batterlike paste. Salt, spices, and starches are added, and then water and corn syrup. The paste is pureed again and then pumped into individual cellulose casings. Then the dogs are given a cold-water bath, at which point the casings are removed. Behold: the hot dog.

QUIET, MUTT!

Q: Okay, so what's in a hush puppy?

A: Have no fear—no real puppies were harmed in the making of your hush puppy. If you've never had this classic food from the American South, hush puppies are deep-fried balls of cornmeal batter, often seasoned with onions or pepper. The most common explanation for the name is that they were originally made by Confederate soldiers while sitting around the camp-fires. They were tossed to hungry, yelping dogs with the command "Hush, puppies!" Over time that became the name of the food. The oldest documented use of the term goes back to a 1918 publication on American English called *Dialect Notes.*

LOAFING AROUND

Q: What did people say was the "greatest thing since sliced bread" before sliced bread?

A: Bread. According to archaeologists, humans have been baking bread for about 30,000 years, and for more than 29,900 of those years, it only came in whole loaves. That all changed in 1928. After tinkering for nearly two decades, an Iowa inventor named Otto Rohwedder perfected his industrial bread-slicing machine. He sold it to the Chillicothe Baking Company, a major bread supplier in the Midwest. And all of a sudden, consumers could buy a loaf of Kleen Maid Sliced Bread.

Except they weren't buying it. People were used to slicing their own bread, which usually came wrapped in a cloth to keep it fresh. They thought presliced bread would go stale faster. So Chillicothe went on a marketing blitz, lauding their "new and improved" product as the "greatest forward step in the baking industry since bread was wrapped." Not only did sliced bread become the norm, but the ads spawned a new phrase: "the greatest thing since sliced bread." So far, no invention has topped that.

BOOZE CLUES

Q: Why isn't there nutrition information on alcohol?

A: Food and alcohol are regulated in the United States by two different government agencies. The Food and Drug Administration controls food, and although alcohol is often classified as a drug, the majority of it is overseen by the Alcohol and Tobacco Tax and Trade Bureau (a division of the Treasury Department).

If the FDA oversees it, it gets the federally mandated nutrition label informing consumers of calories, fat content, carbohydrates, etc. If the Alcohol Bureau controls it, it's technically alcohol, not food, and so it doesn't need nutrition labels…because it isn't food. (Yes, the logic is a bit circular.) However, there is a gray area. Bottled hard cider and gluten-free beer are made with different ingredients than other alcohols, rendering them "foods" by law, and under the jurisdiction of the FDA, which requires that nutrition facts be printed on their labels. Hard cider is made from juice, a food; but gluten-free beer is not made with malted grain, a distinct characteristic of beer, so by that definition it's not alcohol and therefore has to be a food.

NO YOKE

Q: When you eat an egg, are you actually eating a chicken embryo?

A: Sometimes, but it really depends on the type of egg. Free-range eggs sometimes contain embryos, but they're unformed. In order for them to develop into full-fledged chickens, a hen has to incubate it. If the egg is taken away from the bird before she has a chance to warm it with her feathery bottom for around three weeks, the embryo inside remains an undeveloped yolk. On the other hand, factory-farmed eggs remain entirely unfertilized. Modern hens can lay eggs whether they're fertilized or not.

Here's how you can tell if the eggs in your fridge are fertilized. Hold one up to a light source (candles work best). If it appears opaque, it's probably fertilized. Once you crack it open, you'll also probably find red lines running along the egg yolk. Contrary to popular belief, unfertilized eggs taste no different than fertilized ones, and they're equally nutritious. Just try not to think about what might have been.

LET'S TALK TURKEY

Q: Why don't people ever eat turkey eggs?

A: Lots of reasons. Fist, turkeys don't lay nearly as many eggs as do hens (see page 69), and they require a lot more room than hens, so turkey eggs would be much more expensive for farmers to produce. That high cost would be passed on to the consumer.

However, if turkey eggs actually tasted better, farmers might try and sell them, but the truth is, turkey eggs taste horrible. Unlike chicken eggs, which have a lot of water, turkey eggs are mostly dry inside. So when you try to cook a turkey egg, it quickly becomes rubbery and hard to eat.

CRUNCH AND MUNCH

Q: Why do we eat popcorn in movie theaters?

A: Calvin (of *Calvin & Hobbes* fame) once proclaimed, "It's not entertainment if you can't sit in the dark and eat." Americans really seem to enjoy combining those two activities: concession sales account for about 85 percent of a movie theater's profits, and popcorn accounts for most of that.

It's an odd custom when you think about it: while trying to pay attention to what's happening on the screen, movie patrons absentmindedly reach into a bag of $6 popcorn (actual value: a few cents) and then snarf down handful after handful. It's greasy, loud, and not very healthy—especially when you add all that butter. So whose bright idea was it to make popcorn the cornerstone snack at every movie theater from London to Honolulu?

Back in the early days of cinema, eating anything in a theater was frowned upon. The Great Depression changed that. With little money available for more expensive forms of entertainment, Americans flocked to movie theaters (now offering movies with talking!). At the same time, popcorn was becoming a popular—and cheap—snack.

Eager to cash in on both fads at the same time, enterprising vendors started setting up carts with popping machines outside of cinemas. At first, theater owners wouldn't allow patrons to bring the loud, messy snack inside…until they saw there was money to be made. Then the vendors were invited inside, and the rest is snack history.

YOU CAN'T TUNA FISH

Q: **Why is tuna often called "tuna fish"? Is there another kind of tuna it could be confused with?**

A: There are many types of fish that still maintain the "-fish" suffix. In addition to tuna fish, there's catfish and swordfish, for example. Cod was widely called "cod-fish" until the mid-20th century. Trout used to be called "troutfish," too.

It's a holdover from when fish names had other, older meanings. A *cod* was another name for a bag, and *trout* meant "to curdle." Catfish and swordfish got the "-fish" suffix so people wouldn't mistake them for cats or swords. Tuna fish was originally meant to differentiate between…tuna. Fishermen called the entire fish the "tuna," and when it came to its meat, they called that "tunafish," which today we spell as "tuna fish."

SINGING SPIRITS

Q: How do wines have "notes"?

A: Have you ever been to a wine tasting, or read the copy on the back of a wine bottle? If so, then you know that wine has notes. For example, a snooty waiter may inform you, "This full-bodied Chardonnay is heralded as having notes of vanilla and citrus with a walnut finish." This doesn't mean that the wine is infused with vanilla, citrus fruits, or nuts. It's just how our brains (and taste buds) interpret some advanced microchemistry.

Grape juice becomes wine through fermentation. Yeast is added to grapes and grape juice, and it eats the sugar found naturally in the fruit. That, in turn, creates alcohol. Along the way, thousands of complex chemical compounds—still within the grapes—are formed. Even though those compounds are still by and large made of grapes, the molecules have been re-arranged ever so slightly that they taste different from just grape juice or wine. The brain (and taste buds) interprets them as other, more familiar flavors.

For example, let's say that fermentation creates a

chemical compound that has a similar structure to that of apples. Even though the wine is made of grapes, the taste buds will taste that chemical compound, even just a little bit, because the molecules in that compound are arranged like an apple molecule.

BLECCH!

Q: Why does orange juice taste so bad after you brush your teeth?

A: Toothpaste is, among other things, a detergent. And the main ingredient in that detergent is sodium lauryl sulfate. When it gets on your tongue's taste buds, it reduces your ability to taste sweetness and saltiness, and it make sour foods taste bitter. So anything you eat after you brush will not taste as sweet, but few foods or drinks are affected more than orange juice.

BAG MAN

Q: Why are plastic potato chip bags so hard to open?

A: Blame chemist John Spevacek. In a 2012 article called "I'm That Guy," Spevacek wrote that while working for a chemical company that made "multilayer polypropylene films for food packaging," he was given the job of creating a seal strong enough to withstand pressure changes without breaking open—which often happened when cargo trucks carrying bags of chips traveled over the Rocky Mountains. "Other options were technically possible," Spevacek writes, "but not economically feasible. While options exist to prevent premature opening of the bag, such as reducing the initial air pressure in the bag, attempting to add this to the existing processing equipment would have been a nightmare. So it was necessary to increase the seal strength." Good news: potato chip bags don't pop open at high elevations. Bad news: they're very difficult to open at any elevation.

WHOLE FOOD$

Q: Why are organic food products more expensive?

A: After World War II, many governments awarded subsidies to farmers to ensure that the food shortages during the war would not be repeated. These subsidies still exist, but are only given to large-scale farming companies, which leaves out nearly all organic farmers. So basically, your tax dollars have already paid for a portion of the conventionally grown food you buy at the store.

Also, chemical pesticides and fertilizers are less expensive and less time-consuming to use than organic methods. Organic fertilizers made from compost and animal manure are bulkier and more expensive to ship than their chemical counterparts. And for cattle to be considered "organic," they must be given organic feed, which can cost twice as much as conventional feed.

Another factor: whereas organic farmers rotate their crops, conventional farmers grow the same high-yield crop in the same field year after year. As a result, organic farming brings a smaller yield at a higher cost. That cost then gets passed on to grocery stores, because organic farmers can't give grocers the bulk discounts that the big farming companies can.

Grocery stores, in turn, must charge their customers even more for organic food to maintain the same profit margin they get for conventional food. And some grocery stores that cater to more affluent customers charge up to twice as much more for their organic products. Typically, though, the increase ranges from 10 to 40 percent more than conventional foods—meaning if a box of Kellogg's Corn Flakes is $4.00, then a box of organic corn flakes may cost $5.60.

A JUICY QUESTION

Q: What's the difference between apple juice and apple cider?

A: The Simpsons' nerdy neighbor Ned Flanders put it this way: "If it's clear and yellow, you've got juice there, fellow. If it's tangy and brown, you're in cider town." Ned's right, but there's a bit more to it than that.

After apples are freshly picked and then immediately pressed (apples are pressed, not juiced, which makes things confusing when it comes to apple juice), the raw liquid that emerges and is collected is called cider. It's usually bottled as is, unfiltered, cloudy, and brown with particles of apple and other pulpy bits still in the mix. Take that liquid and filter it, and out come most of the solid chunks, thick clouds, and brown color. Then it's pasteurized. The result: apple juice.

The other main difference is yeast. Apple cider contains naturally occurring yeast; it's filtered out of apple juice. That's why apple cider gets fizzier over time, and can even become alcoholic.

That's what technically separates cider and juice, but sometimes the distinction is just a marketing term. There's no federal law that requires juice or cider manufacturers to state if their product is one or the other. The only cider-based law in play here is that hard cider has to be labeled as such because there's alcohol in it, but even that can be apple cider that has naturally gone alcoholic, or apple juice with yeast and sugar added to make it contain alcohol.

SEEMS FISHY

Q: Why do pizzerias offer anchovies if nobody ever orders them?

A: Pizza as we know it today was first developed in the late 18th century in Naples, Italy. Back then, anchovies were a lot more popular than they are now. The little fishes were cheap, plentiful, and thanks to lots of salt and oil, they could be preserved for a long time—which was crucial in the days before refrigeration. So it made sense that anchovies became a popular pizza topping.

When pizza arrived in the United States at the turn

of the 20th century, anchovies remained a popular topping, but they were soon replaced by other spiced meats such as sausage and pepperoni. So why are anchovies still offered? Mostly for nostalgia's sake... and the few people out there who actually like them.

SOME QUESTIONS HAVE NO ANSWERS

"Ever notice the first thing you see at an airport is a big sign that says 'TERMINAL'? Have a nice flight."

—LEWIS GRIZZARD

CURDLED CONUNDRUM

Q: Why is there an expiration date on sour cream?

A: There's a big difference between "spoiled" and "sour." The latter term refers to taste, not its edible state. The souring of the cream is caused by lactic acid bacteria that has been fermented. Those are good bacteria. When the bad bacteria get to it after a certain date, they attack the fats and proteins in the cream, spoiling it for everybody.

ON THE EDGE

Q: **Why are the meat, poultry, and seafood displays almost always along the back of the supermarket?**

A: Meat products are among the most profitable grocery items in the store, so they're placed in such a way that you can see them from every aisle.

MILKING IT

Q: **Why are the dairy products usually as far away from the entrance as possible?**

A: Most everybody buys milk when they shop. To reach it, you've got to walk through a good chunk of the supermarket, often along the perimeter. That's right where the store wants shoppers. The more time you spend shopping along the sides and back of the supermarket, the more money the store makes. About half its profits come from "perimeter" items like fruits and veggies, milk and cheese, and meat, poultry, and fish.

Also, stores like to "anchor" a display by putting popular items at each end. That's why milk, for example, is often at one end of the dairy case and margarine and butter at the other. You've got to run the gauntlet of cheese, yogurt, chips, etc. to get what you came for.

SANKA VERY MUCH

Q: Why are the decaffeinated coffee pots at restaurants orange?

A: People have been drinking coffee for over 500 years, but decaf is only about a century old. It was created in Germany by Ludwig Roselius, who figured out how to use seawater to remove most of the caffeine and still keep the bold taste. The coffee was sold in the U.S. as Sanka, from the French phrase *sans caféine* (without caffeine). General Foods purchased Sanka in 1932 and began aggressively marketing it to restaurants as their default decaf coffee. The company even manufactured special orange coffee pots (which they trademarked as "Sanka Orange") and gave them to restaurants. Their plan was for people to identify the orange coffee pots with decaf. Their plan worked.

MIXED BAG

THE CLOCK STRIKES 13

Q: Why are numbers repeated in modern time telling?

A: Noon is typically referred to as "12 o'clock" in many parts of the English-speaking world. Therefore, it might make sense if the next hour was called "13 o'clock" and so on all the way up to, "Man, I gotta go home, it's way after 23 o'clock!" That might sound weird, but it's equally weird that we just start over after noon. Why is that? And why don't people in the military do it? (They would say, "Man, I gotta get back to base, it's way after twenty-three hundred!")

The civilian system of time telling is typically referred to as the 12-hour clock. While a variation of it dates all the way back to about 1500 B.C., it came into common practice in the 16th century in Europe.

To make things more confusing, early mechanical timepieces in the 14th century often utilized a 24-hour dial. Those were used primarily by astronomers, however. (In the Czech Republic, Prague's famous "orloj" astronomical clock, built in 1410, contains a dial that displays all 24 hours.)

Most people across Europe ended up using the 12-hour clock. That's when a.m. and p.m. were introduced to help clarify what time of day it was. The former is an abbreviation for the Latin *ante meridiem* ("before midday") and the latter for *post meridiem* ("after midday").

But the main reason for this style of timekeeping: it was easier for clockmakers to make a clock face with only 12 hours instead of 24. It would be really difficult to fit 24 hours onto a wristwatch, or to be able to read the time on a 24-hour clock tower.

SOME QUESTIONS HAVE NO ANSWERS

"Opening a can of worms? Do worms even come in cans?"

—ELLEN DEGENERES

HIGHER LEARNING

Q: What's the difference between a college and a university?

A: The terms are used interchangeably, so it gets a little confusing. For example, we generally say, "I'm going to college!" even if the institution is technically, or by name, a university. (Muddling things further: in the UK and Canada, they do the opposite, saying "going to university," even if that university is really a college.)

What's going on here? On the surface, it would make sense that smaller institutions of higher learning are colleges, and larger ones are universities. That's only partially true. By definition, a college is any post–high school institution offering secondary education that awards advanced degrees, be they an associate degree or a bachelor's degree.

A university, however, is a system or collection of colleges, usually in the same physical space (but not always), that operates as a single entity and allows its students to take classes throughout its many colleges. Generally speaking, it's only universities that can award degrees beyond the bachelor's, such as a master's or a doctorate.

MOON UNITS

Q: Why were there moons on outhouse doors?

A: You don't see these old outhouses much anymore, especially near cities—although if you watch old Western movies, they're all over the place. Take a trip to a mining town in Colorado, and you're sure to see one.

Back in the frontier days when outhouses outnumbered indoor toilets, Americans used symbols on the outhouse door to indicate gender, much like today's "male" and "female" signs on public restroom doors. Those are relatively new creations, but in the old days, the most common gendered signs on outhouses were a sunburst for men and a moon for women—both were ancient symbols associated with gender.

However, only the moon symbol remains on outhouses. Why? Ironically, because of its lack of use. Old West towns provided a male outhouse and a female outhouse, but what a lot of them didn't have were many women. Result: the "sun" outhouses got used a lot more and thus didn't last as long. The women's outhouses remained, and soon both genders started using them, so the crescent moon became the de facto symbol.

It's worth noting that the symbols weren't painted on—they were cut out of the door. That let in a little light…and allowed some of the noxious air to escape.

GET A ROOM, ESKIMO

Q: **Do Inuits really kiss by rubbing their noses together, as in the "Eskimo kiss"?**

A: No. That was one of many falsehoods popularized by a 1922 documentary called *Nanook of the North*. In 1920, an American filmmaker named Robert J. Flaherty went to Canada to record the traditional life of the Inuit. The movie was a big hit with Americans who had never seen actual footage of the Inuits' traditional ways. Too bad a lot of them weren't true.

Some of the falsehoods were dictated by necessity: for example, Flaherty built an igloo with an open side so that he'd have enough light to film. Some were dictated by commercial considerations: he renamed the main characters and gave the film's protagonist, an Inuit hunter named Nanook, a replacement wife who was more photogenic than his real one.

Other falsities, though, were completely unnecessary and caused lasting misconceptions. One thing Flaherty made up for no good reason was the "Eskimo kiss," in which two people kiss by rubbing noses. He'd filmed a mother nuzzling her child and reported that the Inuit kissed that way all the time to keep from freezing their mouths together. It wasn't true.

YOU MAD, BARN?

Q: Why are barns red?

A: Today, wooden barns are coated with wood sealant and other preservatives so they will last a long time, but those are 20th-century inventions. Before that, farmers had to cover their barns with a sturdy paint that would seal and protect the wood from the elements. To achieve that, they used linseed oil. The flax-derived oil is orange, so it not only acted as a protectant, but the orange looked good against the green grass and blue sky.

Farmers soon discovered that they could add more ingredients to the linseed oil that would do an even better job, one of which was rust—or, as scientists like to call it, *ferrous oxide*. It's notorious for damaging metal, but when it comes to wood, rust acts as a natural remedy for killing off fungi and invasive mosses. When mixed with the orange linseed oil, the rust turned it into a dark red paint. Today, more sophisticated commercial paints are used, but barns are still mostly painted red. Why? Tradition.

EASY E

Q: Why is the letter E not included in grading?

A: Various methods of grading have been used by schools around the world for centuries. The one employed by most educational centers in the United States dates back to at least 1897 at Mount Holyoke College in Massachusetts. In those days, it was a lot harder to earn an A. That grade only covered scores between 95 and 100 percent, whereas a B represented between 85 and 94 percent. The students who earned scores between 75 and 84 percent got Cs and, as strange as it might sound, Ds were set aside for those who hit the 75 percent mark. Anyone who scored below that number earned an E.

A year later, university officials decided to bump E up a notch and add F, which stood for "failure." The system proved popular and spread quickly to colleges and other schools across the country. Gradually, the E was phased out because some of the students thought it stood for "excellent." The E was all but gone by 1930.

GUILTY MINUS THE GUILT

Q: What does pleading "no contest" in a trial mean? Is it the same as pleading guilty?

A: If you've been charged with a crime and you have to enter a plea in court, you can enter "not guilty," which will grant you a trial to prove your innocence. If you plead guilty, however, you're still given a trial. Why? Because the prosecution still has to prove you did it in order to make sure that you're not taking the rap for someone else, or you're not mentally unstable.

But there's a third plea option: "no contest." You're saying that you are willing to take the punishment that a guilty verdict would have netted…without a trial.

That's not necessarily an admission of guilt, but most people who use this tactic know that they won't be found innocent.

So why do it? The main reason is that the accused fears that a lengthy trial will drag their name through the mud. If they plead not guilty and are found guilty, their penalty will often be much stiffer than if they had pleaded no contest. It also means they get out of paying expensive lawyer fees.

Another reason people plead no contest: it may help them in a civil suit in the future. For example, if you harmed someone by driving drunk, and you're found guilty, then the injured party can later sue you based on that conviction. But if you plead no contest, there's no conviction that could be used as evidence of guilt in a civil trial.

Those most likely to plead no contest are usually celebrities who would like to avoid a PR-damaging court case.

THE HAPPIEST BASKET-BALL COURT ON EARTH

Q: Is there really a basketball court at the top of the Matterhorn in Disneyland?

A: "Matterhorn Bobsleds" is still one of the most popular attractions at the original Disneyland in Anaheim, California. The mountain's first bobsleds began racing down its "icy slopes" in the spring of 1959. Back then, it was among the most sophisticated theme park rides in the world. Unlike similar roller coasters, it was housed inside a colossal, 147-foot-tall overlay constructed to resemble the real Matterhorn in the Swiss Alps.

The ride (and its animatronic Abominable Snowman) currently occupy the lower half of the structure. The remainder contains a break room, an engine that propels the bobsleds to the top of the track, and a stairwell that leads to the peak. There also happens to be a basketball hoop (and a free-throw line) located near the bottom of the stairs.

That hoop led to this popular urban legend. It goes like this: Walt Disney himself added the basketball court in order to skirt a local law that prevented anything other than sports arenas from being built above a certain height. But that's not true, and one hoop and a free-throw line doesn't make a whole basketball court, but the rumor still won't seem to go away. For the record, the hoop was added by one of the "mountain climbers" who entertains Disneyland's crowds by scaling the Matterhorn on afternoons when it isn't too windy.

OY VEY CAN YULE SEE?

Q: Why do so many Jewish people—particularly in the United States—eat Chinese food on Christmas?

A: Christmas is a federal holiday in the U.S., and most businesses and restaurants close so their employees can be with their families. That's great for people who celebrate Christmas, but for people of other faiths, it's just another day (except that almost nothing is open).

However, one kind of business has been open on Christmas Day for more than a century: Chinese restaurants. Since Christianity wasn't nearly as popular in China as it was in the West, Christmas wasn't celebrated by most first-generation Chinese immigrants.

For Jews living in New York City's Lower East Side at the turn of the 20th century, it was match made in, well…maybe not heaven, but the two disparate cultures—which happened to be New York's two largest immigrant groups at the time—began a tradition that continues today.

One of the reasons this relationship works so well is due to the similarities between Jewish food and American-style Chinese food: lots of fried things, for example, and it's easy for Jews to obey the kosher dietary law of not mixing meat and dairy because Chinese food is mostly free of dairy products. And finally, Chinese food tastes good. (Just hold the pork.)

SPORTS

JUST ONE OF THE GUYS

Q: **Why do baseball managers wear uniforms?**

A: Baseball is weird. It's the only sport where the players who are trying to score don't even touch the ball. Another quirk: unlike the coaches of other professional sports teams—who wear street clothes—baseball managers suit up just like the players. This custom goes back to the early days of the game when most managers were also players, so they had to wear their uniforms to play. That was generally not the case for early basketball, hockey, and football coaches. Although baseball player-managers had become scarce by the mid-20th century (Pete Rose of the 1986 Reds was the last), the tradition of wearing the uniform remains.

Two managers, Connie Mack of the Philadelphia Athletics from 1901 to 1950, and Burt Shotton of the Brooklyn Dodgers in the late 1940s, went against tradition by wearing suits during the games. The official rules say that "coaches" (as in the first- and third-base coaches) must wear uniforms. Although they are the equivalent of coaches in other sports, baseball managers are managers, and, therefore, are not held to this rule.

SOME QUESTIONS HAVE NO ANSWERS

"What's the shelf life of a shelf?"

—JASON LOVE

GIMME FIVE

Q: **Why do baseball games begin at five minutes after the hour or half hour, at times like 1:05 or 7:35?**

A: When radio stations started broadcasting baseball games, radio shows were already timed to start and end on the hour or half hour, so having the games start at five minutes after gave stations time for ads, for the announcers to talk about the game to be played, and, since 1941, for the national anthem to be played.

But not *all* games start at five after: Toronto Blue Jays home games begin at seven minutes after, and some other teams start games at 10 or even 15 after, and afternoon games often start at five minutes *before* the hour. In 2006, the Chicago White Sox signed a three-year, $500,000 sponsorship deal to change the times of their 7:05 games to begin at 7:11. (Guess who they made the deal with?)

TOUCHING BASE

Q: **Why is home plate shaped differently than the other bases?**

A: From 1869 to 1900, home plate was a 16-inch square (the other bases are 15-inch squares), positioned with one corner pointed at the pitcher. That made it difficult for both the pitcher and the umpire to pinpoint the strike zone, so in 1900 the baseball rules committee changed it to the five-sided shape that's still used today, with its square bottom, 17 inches across, and the bottom, or flat part, closest to the pitcher. When viewed from above, it kind of looks like a house. **Bonus Fact:** Before 1869, home plate was a 12-inch circle made of wood, cast iron, marble, or even a dinner plate—which is why we call it "home plate."

ORANGE YOU GLAD TO SEE ME?

Q: **Why are basketballs orange?**

A: The color of balls used in various sporting events has a lot to do with the surface they're played on, and how well they can be seen over the top of that surface. For example, a white baseball shows up best against a green field and a blue sky, and a black hockey puck shows up best on the white ice.

These same rules apply to basketball. In the early days of the sport (invented by Canadian James Naismith in 1891), the balls were typically brown. But as basketball became more popular, spectators had a tough time seeing a brown ball dribbled across a wooden floor. Even the players themselves had a hard time seeing the ball.

That all changed in 1957 thanks to Tony Hinkle, coach of Butler University's basketball team in Indiana. He challenged the Spalding Company to come up with something better. Their solution: an orange basketball. It was officially used for the first time during an NCAA game in 1958. And it worked so well that orange has been the norm ever since.

There have been a few notable exceptions, though. The American Basketball Association used patriotic red, white, and blue balls during its nine seasons. And today, the WNBA uses an orange-and-white ball.

WHAT'S THE MATTER, TENNIS BALL? SCARED?

Q: Why are tennis balls yellow?

A: Like basketball in the previous question, the reason for this is so the ball can be seen better…but not by the players themselves, or even people in the stands. Before the 1970s, tennis balls where white, and no one complained about their color. But when tennis became popular enough for it to be televised, viewers had a tough time seeing the white balls zoom across their screens (picture quality back then left much to be desired). So after experimenting with several different colors, in 1972, the International Tennis Federation made the switch to what is called "fluorescent yellow" or "optic yellow."

FUZZY LOVE

Q: Why are tennis balls fuzzy ?

A: The fastest tennis serves can top speeds of 160 mph,

but if the balls weren't fuzzy, those serves would be even faster. The extra surface area not only creates more resistance against the air, but it makes the ball softer and bounce less. Also, when the ball meets the racket, the fuzz allows the strings to "hold onto it" longer, giving the player more control over the direction and spin. In short: the fuzz adds precision to the game.

THE OTHER FOOTBALL

Q: Why is soccer called "football" outside of the United States?

A: They ask the same question (but reversed) in other countries: "Why do Americans call it 'soccer'?" Everywhere else, the sport that features kicking a round ball with your foot is called football.

The sport we know of as soccer dates back to at least the first century B.C., whereas the sport we know of as American football was created in the 1860s at Yale University in Connecticut. It was based on rugby, which was invented a few decades earlier in the town of Rugby, England, when a football player picked up the ball and started running with it.

But there was some confusion, because at first, rugby was also called football in England. So to make a distinction between the two, the traditional sport with the round ball became known as "association football," and the other one, which used an oblong ball, was called "rugby football." Shortened versions soon appeared: "soccer" from the "soc" in "association," and "rugger" for rugby (which some still call it today). So the word "soccer" is actually a British term. That was the primary name for the sport in England for more than a century. When American football became popular in the early 20th century, Americans stuck with the British word "soccer."

In the late 1970s, soccer really took off in popularity in the United States. That's when the Brits began to "disassociate" themselves with the term "soccer" and began referring to it by its original name: football.

NECESSARY ROUGHNESS

Q: Why do football players wear lots of padding but rugby players don't?

A: If you ask most rugby players, they'll say it's because "American footballers are wimps." No comment on the veracity of that statement, but it is true that the two games, though similar in how they're played, have vastly different uniforms. Football players wear a hard helmet and thick padding over their shoulders and upper legs, whereas rugby players wear little more than a pair of shorts and a jersey. And these big, strong men can tackle each other just as hard as football players can.

However, there's a lot less tackling in rugby...and a lot more running. If you've never seen a rugby game, it kind of looks like soccer, but instead of kicking the ball, the players carry it down the field and pass or drop-kick it to each other. Unlike in football, they don't stop between plays—it's just run, run, run until someone gets tackled or makes a "try" (similar to a touchdown in football).

Without a helmet and pads to protect rugby players, they (in theory) take fewer risks and tend to be more strategic when it comes to physical contact. In contrast, many people blame the inordinate amount of concussions in football on the helmet and all that padding—it allows players to hit each other much harder than they would without them. In rugby, concussions aren't the main concern—spinal injuries are.

That's not to say that rugby players don't wear *any* protective gear. Many wear mouth guards and shoulder pads. Most leagues, however, have rules that prevent the pads from being thicker than about ⅓ inch. They also have to remain hidden beneath the players' jerseys. Some leagues also allow players to wear "scrum caps" to protect their ears during scrums, a tactic that involves players packing themselves together while scrambling to gain possession of the ball. **Bonus Fact:** Rugby scrums are so intense that, over time, players can develop what's commonly referred to as "cauliflower ear." This nasty condition leads to cartilage separating from connective tissue and slowly dying, eventually causing the outer ear to become swollen and deformed…like a cauliflower.

STOP AND GO

Q: **An NFL football game lasts 60 minutes. How much of that time are they actually playing football?**

A: If you used a stopwatch to tally up the actual playing time during a three-hour football broadcast, it would total about 11 minutes. Actual playing time is measured from the snap or kick of the ball to the whistle at the end of the play.

So what fills the rest of the time? About 20 minutes are spent watching replays. Another 20 or so minutes are spent watching canned video features, cheerleaders, coaches, crowd shots, halftime, and pre- and post-game chatter. Another hour is spent watching the players stand around and huddle up between plays, which still leaves an hour. That's for all the commercials.

COMMERCIAL RACING

Q: Why are NASCAR cars covered with ads?

A: In 1972, a year after losing the right to advertise tobacco products on television, the tobacco company R. J. Reynolds tried a new marketing tactic by sponsoring the first Winston Cup NASCAR racing series (now called the Sprint Cup). In the mid-1970s, partial races were telecast on ABC's *Wide World of Sports*, giving NASCAR a wider audience.

But its biggest boost came with the 1979 Daytona 500, the first NASCAR race broadcast live on national television. On a day when the northeastern U.S. was paralyzed by a snowstorm, millions of TV viewers watched the race—which ended in a dramatic wreck on the final lap, followed by a fistfight between Cale Yarborough and Donnie Allison. The race was big news and drew huge ratings.

Seeing dollar signs, more companies jumped on the sponsorship bandwagon, creating a marriage of convenience: stock cars make perfect blank slates for ads, and stock car racing is so expensive that teams can't do it week after week without the money they receive from sponsors. How much money? A company can shell out up to $35 million just to plaster its logo onto one race car.

Bonus Fact: NASCAR's global TV audience per race is about six million viewers. That's chump change compared to Formula One's: 150 million.

FLAG PARADE

Q: What do the colored flags mean in NASCAR?

A: If the flag is green, that means "the race is on." A yellow flag means "caution"—there's a wreck ahead (no driver may pass any other while the yellow flag is up). A red flag means "stop now"—there's a really *bad* wreck ahead. A red flag with a yellow "X" means that "pit road is closed," usually because a wreck occurred there. A black flag is used to tell a specific driver to "return to pit road," which usually means that he or she has violated a rule, or the officials have spotted a mechanical problem on the car. A white flag means "one lap to go." Then the mad dash begins for NASCAR's most sought-after piece of fabric—the checkered flag!

AT WORK

BAD COP, NO DONUT!

Q: Where did the "cops like to eat donuts" stereotype come from?

A: The cliché is as strong as ever: just look at Chief Wiggum on *The Simpsons* chomping on a donut. The cops in the 2012 animated film *Wreck-It Ralph* are literally walking donuts.

The concept dates back to the 1930s. Before the proliferation of fast-food restaurants and convenience stores on every corner, there weren't a lot of places for swing shift or overnight workers to get a bite to eat or a cup of coffee. By and large, pre–World War II American restaurants opened shortly before normal breakfast hours (maybe 5:00 or 6:00 a.m.) and closed shortly after traditional dinner hours (around 8:00 or 9:00 p.m.). Sure, there were all-night diners, but cops can be called away at any time and may not be able to wait around for their food to be served.

The only other establishments that were open at all hours: donut shops. Beat cops could easily pop in for a snack and a cup of coffee and be on their way. So it became a common sight to see a police car parked at a donut shop, hence the stereotype. (Another mitigating factor: donuts are delicious.)

> ## SOME QUESTIONS HAVE NO ANSWERS
>
> **"Can a blue man sing the whites?"**
>
> **—ALGIS JUODIKIS**

MIDHUSBAND?

Q: **What do you call a male midwife?**

A: A midwife. This occupation is primarily made up of women who aid other women in childbirth, but there are several dozen male midwives officially certified in the United States, and many more exist around the world. So why aren't they called "midhusbands"? Because the "wife" in the term refers to the woman giving birth, not the person helping her. It was derived from a Middle English term that meant "with wife" or "with woman."

I MADE A TYPE-OW

Q: **What is a carpal tunnel anyway, and how can typing at a keyboard damage it?**

A: The carpal tunnel is literally a tunnel inside your wrist that's made of bones and connective tissue. And there's a lot squeezed in there, including nine flexor tendons and the median nerve, which extends from your shoulder down your arm, through the carpal tunnel, and then to your thumb and first three fingers. That tunnel is very narrow, so if any of the tendons become swollen, they press up against the median nerve, leading to carpal tunnel syndrome (CTS).

If you sit at a desk and type for a living, then you're at risk, especially if you don't have good posture and let your hands hang below your wrists when you type.

Over time, those nine tendons get pinched inside the carpal tunnel and can become swollen, which damages the median nerve. Symptoms include numbness, tingling, and pain in the hands, fingers, and wrists. Doctors recommend that you type with both feet firmly placed on the floor. There's also ergonomic equipment such as keyboards and mouse pads with built-in "wrist rests" that can also help.

More than three million Americans are diagnosed with CTS each year. But typing isn't the only repetitive motion that can cause it. Mechanics and artists can get it, as can retail or factory workers who use their hands to do the same thing over and over. If you're at risk, doctors recommend stretching your fingers and doing other isometric exercises, along with taking plenty of breaks.

Bonus Fact: CTS isn't caused solely by repetitive motion. Other factors and triggers can damage the median nerve—including obesity, oral contraceptives, hypothyroidism, arthritis, diabetes, prediabetes (impaired glucose tolerance), and trauma.

CAN'T TEACH THIS

Q: Can tenured professors really not get fired?

A: The concept of tenure is widely misunderstood. It's a privilege that is bestowed upon high-performing or well-respected college professors after many years of work. Tenure is usually officially granted at three, five, or seven years, depending on the institution. It's sought after by academics, and carefully doled out by administrators, because it means job security in an often-insecure field.

But it's not absolute job security. Tenure guarantees a job for those who have it, but only if the job is available. For example, if a college's biology department cuts its faculty from 15 to 12 spots, the 12 spots would be filled from a list of the most tenured instructor on down until the positions are filled. It's a fancy, collegiate form of "last hired, first fired."

The notion that tenure gives a professor free reign to do whatever he or she wants without consequence is a myth. That's because the other major benefit of tenure is that it grants the holder a fair hearing, rather than outright termination, should there be any allegations of wrongdoing. Even then, those accusations must be proved with substantial evidence that the professor did something wrong. Tenured professors get a "fair shot," but they aren't invincible.

BOXED IN

Q: What depraved individual invented the office cubicle, and why?

A: The cubicle—as it was first envisioned—was actually a revolutionary approach to creating a more fun and productive work environment for bosses and employees alike. Before cubicles, most desk workers, or "pencil pushers" as they were called after entering the workforce in the 1950s, sat in giant rooms full of rows of desks laid out in a grid, all facing the same direction. The average pencil pusher's view: the back of a fellow worker's head. An American inventor named Bob Propst called this setup a "vast wasteland…that saps vitality, blocks talent, frustrates accomplishment."

In 1960, he set out to change that. He interviewed office workers and bosses and then worked with a furniture company to create "Action Office." The first design, released in 1964, was a single, freestanding piece of furniture that included bins and a few shelves on each side. The floor units attached to partition walls that could be joined to each other in different configurations. Each desk was surrounded by three attachable dividers, or walls, which were high enough to give some privacy but not so high that the worker couldn't stand up and see the rest of the workroom (a practice that would later be called "prairie dogging").

These new, spacious workplaces took over corporate America. In the 1980s, when the digital revolution took hold, the Action Office system (and the dozens of copycats that followed) could easily fit a computer, monitor, and printer. Sure, those early computers were much larger than today's sleek PCs and Macs, but the Action Office was spacious enough to handle them. At least that's how it was supposed to work.

But as office rents skyrocketed in the 1990s, employers were forced to accommodate more workers in smaller areas. Ironically, the feature that made it so easy to give these workers more space—adjustable walls—also gave bosses an easy way to cram more and more cubicles together. Result: the wide angles of the Action Office closed up and became squares, and the area of the average workspace was reduced to 8 square feet. (It's even smaller today.) The grid of desks had returned, only now they had fabric-covered walls between them.

Only 20 years after partitioned offices ushered in a new era of comfort and productivity, cubicles (as they were being called) came to symbolize everything that was wrong with the American workplace. Bob Propst was demoralized by what his grand idea had become: "The dark side of this is that not all organizations are intelligent and progressive. Lots are run by crass people who take the same kind of equipment and create hellholes. They make little bitty cubicles and stuff people in them. Barren, rat-hole places."

YOU'RE FIRED!

Q: Why are people fired with a pink slip?

A: The phrase is a euphemism—although not a very comforting one—for "getting fired." Usually, companies don't provide a little piece of paper letting you know you're fired because your boss just tells you that you're canned. But once upon a time, sacked employees found out they were sacked when they received a pink slip in their pay envelope.

"Pink slip," both the phrase and the action, most likely began in vaudeville, the theatrical entertainment circuit of the early 20th century. Thousands of acts were booked at theaters throughout North America via the United Booking Office. When they had to cancel an act, they'd send the unlucky performer a notice on pink paper—a can't-miss shade.

Over the course of the 20th century, more and more businesses adopted triplicate forms for official business, and the pink slip survived. When an employee was processed by a company for termination, the paperwork was filled out in triplicate—white, yellow, and pink. The white and yellow went elsewhere in the company, while the pink went to the employee, in their pay envelope, during their last week on the job.

BUSINESS

PROOF OF PARADOX

Q: **How can you participate in a product's "no pur-chase necessary" contest when you have to send in a "proof of purchase" in order to enter the contest?**

A: This curious conundrum is the result of some compli-cated federal broadcasting laws. Under U.S. Federal Communications Commission rules, national lotteries are illegal. When a company is giving away a prize as a means to promote its brand—such as a "look under the cap and win" sweepstakes from Coca-Cola—it has to carefully obey that law. In fact, there are three ques-tions a company must answer if it wishes to broadcast or promote the contest on TV or the radio, a process the FCC calls "consideration":

1) Is a prize being offered?
2) Is chance involved?
3) Does something have to be purchased to win the prize?

A promotional contest generally would have to answer "yes" to the first two questions, as prizes are offered and chance is most certainly involved (most winners are chosen at random). It's that third clause that's the sticking point: of course, companies holding contests want consumers to buy something before they participate in the contest—it's the whole point of the contest, after all. But if in the commercials for the contest the company states "no purchase necessary," then it no longer qualifies as a lottery and can proceed.

BIG MONEY

Q: Can you cash a giant novelty check?

A: You just won the Publishers Clearinghouse sweep-stakes! Congratulations! Better sign the back of that gigantic $2 million check the TV crew surprised you with.

One problem: that isn't actually the check you're supposed to take to the bank and cash. It's merely a cardboard prop used for photo ops. Why so big? It makes for better TV. Besides, big money winners are paid an annuity—a percentage of the money in a check every year for 20 years (or whatever the rules stipulate).

But wait—that giant novelty check isn't necessarily *not* a viable check. Checks are made at a standard size so they can be processed by banks in volume at great speed. But in reality, a check itself is merely a "formal representation," or promise, that funds will be trans-ferred from one party to another. Legally, a check can be made out on anything—a piece of cardboard, a napkin, a banana, and there's even a story about a farmer who once used the side of his cow as a check—as long as it contains a bank account number, bank routing number, the amount due, the date, and a signature. So if all that stuff were written on a giant novelty check, you can take it to the bank. (You'll probably have to wait in line for the teller, as most novelty checks won't fit in a standard ATM.)

A STEAL OF A DEAL

Q: How did those "eight albums for a penny" record clubs work?

A: Millions of music lovers built up their collections in the 1980s and 1990s by responding to a magazine ad from Columbia House, BMG, or other, similar services offering "eight albums for a penny." How on earth was that a viable business model? Easy: many of their tactics were quasi-legal.

If you ever ordered one of the eight essentially free albums, you were really signing up for a subscription music service. Columbia House would send you an album of the month…unless you sent back a little card specifically asking the company *not* to send it. What? You forgot about the card? Or you lost it? Too bad, because you're going to get an album you didn't want but have to pay for…at a cost far above retail. In the early 1990s, a Columbia House CD of the month cost $17.95 (plus shipping), about five bucks more than it cost at the mall. This is called "negative option billing," and it's now illegal in many states and jurisdictions.

Adding to the underhanded tactics, instead of obtaining expensive licenses with the major record labels, the clubs would just sell the albums they wanted to sell and then give the record labels a slightly higher than normal royalty rate. When challenged legally, the clubs' attorneys argued that since the labels cashed the checks they sent, the licensing agreement was implied. Or, if a label complained, the clubs would stop carrying that company's product.

Another way the clubs cut their costs to increase their profit: none of the tapes, records, and CDs they sold were "official" copies. They weren't quite bootlegs, either. Instead, Columbia House and BMG would rent or buy the master recordings of albums and produce their own copies, dirt-cheap. They'd cut corners by not including liner notes with CDs, or simplifying the artwork on the discs. What you ended up with were a bunch of really cheap products that you probably paid a lot more than a penny for.

SOME QUESTIONS HAVE NO ANSWERS

"Why do people say, 'It's always the last place you look'? Of course it is. Why would you keep looking after you've found it?"

—BILLY CONNOLLY

DOUBLE THEIR PLEASURE

Q: Why do late-night commercials always offer to throw in a second, identical product "at no extra cost"?

A: Because it's a scam. Those products you see breathlessly hyped on late-night TV are produced for next to nothing overseas and then marketed to Americans at extremely marked-up prices. By touting them as brand-new products that "aren't sold in stores," companies fool gullible consumers into believing they can get a great product for very little money. "Operators are standing by. Call now!"

One of the main ways this "direct response television," as it's called, makes a profit is on the shipping and handling. Buried in the very fast talking, or the fine print that blinks on and off the screen at the end of the commercial, is the fact that shipping and handling costs a lot more than you might think. It also says that shipping can take six to ten weeks. That means the company pays very little for shipping via the "slow boat from China" bulk rate.

So if you finally gave in and ordered that Miracle Toe-Cheese Scraper®, here's the rundown: it cost the company about a buck to produce and even less to package and ship, but you paid $19.99 for it (because the commercial told you that similar toe-cheese scrapers sell for more than $50 at retail stores). The worst part: that $19.99 doesn't even include their completely arbitrary "shipping and handling" cost. That's another $8.

"But wait—order in the next 15 minutes and we'll send you a second Miracle Toe-Cheese Scraper® at no extra cost!" Sometimes they add on "as long as you pay the shipping and handling," and sometimes they don't. Either way, it means they get to tack on another $8 "shipping and handling" fee. So you may have thought you were getting two awesome toe-cheese scrapers for $20, but what you actually get—six to ten weeks later—are two crappy toe-cheese scrapers for $36. And it's all legal—just look at the fine print.

STOP MAKING CENTS

Q: Does it really cost more than a penny to make a penny?

A: Yes. A report released by the United States Government Accountability Office in December 2015 indicated that it costs about 1.7 cents to manufacture a single penny. Reason: the rising price of metals. To cut costs, the U.S. Mint started using zinc and coating pennies with copper in 1982. Unfortunately, the value of zinc has also increased over the past several decades. Despite their copper color, zinc comprises about 97.5% of every modern penny. Meanwhile, making a nickel costs 8 cents.

So why not switch to a cheaper material? It's estimated that the government could save $39 million annually if it figured out another way to make both coins, but there's another problem to consider. Doing so would force businesses that own and maintain vending machines and similar coin-operated gadgets to refit them with new slots and new interior mechanics. That would cost businesses somewhere between $2.4 billion and $10 billion. So Americans are stuck with pennies and nickels for the time being. But good news if you're Canadian—the penny is being phased out there!

SPEND A PENNY

Q: Why do the English call them "pennies," and Americans call them "cents" (and "pennies")?

A: Because once upon a time, way before the Beatles, Americans absolutely hated the English and their monarchist government. That's why they revolted in the late 18th century to form an independent country based on democratic principles. During the American Revolution, an American diplomat named Gouverneur Morris tried to "Americanize" the language, so he lobbied to change the British word "penny" to "cent" (which is a prefix meaning a hundred, as in "centimeter" and "century") to denote that it is one-hundredth of a dollar. Morris was only partially successful, as both terms are used interchangeably in the U.S. today.

FIZZY FEUD

Q: Why did Coca-Cola mess with its time-tested formula and create New Coke in the 1980s?

A: If you were around at the time, you may remember the great "Cola Wars" of the 1970s and 1980s between PepsiCo and the Coca-Cola Company. It was really big news at the time, as both soda giants vied for carbonated sugar water supremacy. PepsiCo took the opening shot in 1975 with "The Pepsi Challenge." First set up in shopping malls, and then made into a series of TV commercials, the challenge featured blindfolded consumers taking a sip of each beverage and then noting which one they preferred. Most of them picked Pepsi. Why? It was a bit sweeter, and studies showed that, when given a choice between two small helpings of food (in this case, a sip of pop), people will instinctively choose the sweeter one.

So in 1985, Coca-Cola took a huge gamble by tinkering with its decades-old formula, creating a slightly sweeter version called New Coke.

The response was overwhelmingly negative. Within days, Coca-Cola's Atlanta headquarters were receiving 1,500 angry calls a day from people who absolutely *hated* the new drink. (The company had a psychiatrist listen in on the calls, and he said that many of them were comparable to "the death of a family member.") Comedians and talk-show hosts derided New Coke. "Coke's decided to make their formula sweeter," quipped David Letterman, "How? They're going to mix it with Pepsi." Even Cuban president Fidel Castro called New Coke a "sign of American capitalist decadence."

PepsiCo took advantage of the debacle with an ad blitz making fun of New Coke—it enjoyed some of its biggest profits ever as millions of consumers switched brands. Less than a year later, Coca-Cola re-released its original formula as "Classic Coke," and sales started to rebound. New Coke limped along until it was quietly renamed "Coca-Cola II" in 1992. It was phased out for good in 2002.

So after all was said and done, who was victorious in the Cola Wars? In 1996, *Fortune* magazine declared that, based on total sales, the winner was Coca-Cola. But the New Coke debacle is still taught about in marketing classes as one of the costliest blunders in business history.

SOME QUESTIONS HAVE NO ANSWERS

"How come aspirins are packed in child-proof containers, but bullets just come in a box?"

—JAY LENO

ENTERTAINMENT

'TIS A BIRTHDAY WHICH I SEE BEFORE ME?

Q: **When is William Shakespeare's birthday?**

A: Shakespeare may be history's most celebrated writer, but many aspects of his life remain a mystery. The Bard's birthday is usually observed on April 23, but that date amounts to a guess. A church record states that he was baptized on April 26, 1564, in the English town of Stratford-upon-Avon. So he may have been born a few days prior to that, or even a few weeks. Of course, had they known that this newborn would grow up to become the most famous wordsmith in the Western world, his birth might have been reported. But alas, he was just a baby.

If April 23 is the correct birth date, it creates a chilling coincidence: as Hamlet himself might put it, the Bard "shuffled off this mortal coil" at the age of 52 in 1616…on April 23.

THE BARD TRUTH

Q: **Did Shakespeare really write all those plays?**

A: History tells us that William Shakespeare authored 36 plays, 154 sonnets, and two narrative poems between 1588 and 1616. But as you learned in the previous question, little is known about the man himself, and no manuscripts written in his own hand have ever been found. This fact has inspired speculation by pseudo-scholars, cranks, and English society snobs that Shakespeare—the commoner son of a glovemaker—couldn't have been intelligent or educated enough to write "his own" works. He wrote in detail about distant lands, but no record exists of him ever leaving England.

Why would the real author have given the credit to Shakespeare? One theory: many of the plays dealt with members of the English royal family and were politically controversial. The real William Shakespeare, according to this theory, was a third-rate actor, playwright, and theater gadfly who was more than happy to take credit for work he was not capable of producing.

Whatever the case, several other people (including Queen Elizabeth I and a Catholic pope) have been proposed as the real Shakespeare. The most popular theory: Sir Francis Bacon, who kept his identity a secret to protect his reputation, as well as his standing in the royal court. Since a number of the plays dealt with English monarchs, he paid Shakespeare, a no-body, to take the credit. Shakespeare's supporters, however, say there's no hard evidence that anyone other than the Bard wrote the plays and poems.

DIM BULBS

Q: Why are movies referred to as the "silver screen"?

A: Early "moving picture shows," though primitive by today's standards, were considered cutting-edge technology in the 1910s. Audiences were wowed by what they saw…when they could see it. The problem was, film projector lightbulbs had very low wattage, so when the movies were projected onto a white screen, the picture looked dark and foggy. Theater owners knew something had to be done when unimpressed patrons started demanding their nickel back (which was worth a lot more a century ago).

The solution: silver-colored screens made of silk or synthetic fiber made the images appear brighter and crisper. Some theaters instead opted to cover their screens in reflective, metallic paint to accomplish the same goal, while others coated them in a thin layer of silver dust. They all, to varying degrees, had the same effect: a better picture. By the 1920s, people were using the phrase "silver screen" to describe movies in general.

WHY. DON'T. YOU. COME. UP. AND. SEE. ME.

Q: Why do old movie stars talk in that stilted, theatrical way?

A: Up until the late 1960s, when gritty realism became the dominant style of American film, Hollywood movies had a high level of theatrics and artifice. The actors all seemed to talk like…they were in a film, using a stilted speaking style seldom heard outside of a movie theater. Today, it's most associated with Katharine Hepburn or Cary Grant, but from the 1930s to the 1960s, most movie stars spoke in a clipped, R-dropping, well-projected, vaguely upper-crust British accent, whether they were British (like Grant) or American (like Hepburn).

It's called the Mid-Atlantic English accent, and it's an affectation, not an organic, geographical-based accent. It's a hybrid of mannered British English and standard American English—hence the name "Mid-Atlantic" (which would technically put it in the middle of the ocean, but that's not important right now). This speaking style was the result of elocution and refinement lessons in prep schools on both sides of the ocean, not to mention acting schools. Film directors liked the accent because it conveyed class, linking it in the minds of American audiences to the theater, or fancy Brits...while remaining just American enough.

Another reason for the speaking style: classic Hollywood actors actually spoke louder. Most of them came from a theater background, where you have to project your voice and speak clearly so everyone in the audience can hear you. Early recording technology wasn't as sensitive as it is today, so actors had to make sure their lines were clear enough to cut through the hiss of early tape. When technology advanced in the late 1960s, and directors like Woody Allen and Robert Altman attempted to bring more realism to the theater experience, actors started talking like real people (good actors, anyway).

SOME QUESTIONS HAVE NO ANSWERS

"Do Lipton employees take coffee breaks?"

—STEVEN WRIGHT

YOUR FRIEND IN TIME

Q: How did Doc and Marty get to be such good buddies in the *Back to the Future* trilogy?

A: The friendship between Doctor Emmett Brown and Marty McFly (Christopher Lloyd and Michael J. Fox) is a bit weird if you think about it. The 1985 movie never gives Doc's age, but it's implied that he's in his 60s or early 70s. Meanwhile, Marty is only 17. How many teenagers do you know who hang out with wacky old scientists?

The origin of their friendship, though never explained in the films, was finally revealed in the first issue of an official *Back to the Future* comic book series that debuted in 2015. After a bully named Needles (played by Red Hot Chili Peppers member Flea in the movies) demands that Marty find him a replacement tube for his guitar amp, he's forced to take desperate measures.

Marty discovers that the only music shop in Hill Valley has sold all of their tubes to Doc for an experiment, so he decides to break into the inventor's laboratory to steal one. The clever high school student manages to overcome a series of booby traps, but he's eventually captured by the crafty inventor. Marty confesses that he was trying to steal from him and, impressed with his ingenuity and honesty, Doc offers him a job as his assistant (and one of the tubes as well, so he won't get pounded by Needles). The rest is movie history.

JUDGE AND JUDY

Q: Are TV courtroom shows legally binding?

A: A verdict of an order to pay damages on *Judge Judy* or *The People's Court* is legally binding inasmuch as a contract is a legally binding document. The "trials" that air on these TV court shows, however, are not real trials. But they are real cases that are usually brought over from small-claims courts.

TV court show producers track down litigants with cases pending in small-claims courts in California and New York. Is it because those states have laws that allow for cases to be argued on television? Nope—it's because that's where TV shows are produced, and also because those states are heavily populated, and the court systems welcome court shows relieving them of a few cases from their huge backlogs. Litigants agree to argue their cases on television, in turn, because the TV show offers a guaranteed quick solution to their case. (And hey, who doesn't want to be on TV?)

The cases are presented with all the trappings of a real courtroom trial, but legally speaking, these affairs are *arbitration*. By definition, arbitration isn't court; it's an alternative to court, a way to settle a case outside of a trial. Both parties in a case present their side to an arbitrator, who then delivers a legally binding decision. The arbitrator doesn't have to be a judge, but they usually are—for example, Judge Judy Sheindlin was a New York criminal judge, and the show *Judge Mathis* stars a retired superior court judge of Michigan's 36th

District Court, Greg Mathis.

Like any arbitrator's decision, a TV judge's decision is legally binding, but not under the threat of jail time or fines. The litigants are contracted to the court show's production company and agree to adhere to the final ruling. Nevertheless, winners and losers both get an appearance fee for being on TV, which generally covers any damage payments the loser may be ordered to pay out.

FREE PARKING

Q: **How come TV and movie characters always get a parking spot right in front of the building?**

A: There are few things more aggravating than trying to find a place to park on a crowded city street. You circle the block, still can't find a spot, so you pull into a parking garage, go up and up to the third level, and then try to squeeze into a tiny spot between a giant column and a giant SUV. It's not only frustrating, but it would be quite boring to watch. And that's the reason why most movie and TV characters have this seemingly supernatural ability to find a spot right out front of where they need to be: to keep the story going. After all, would you really want to watch the *Millennium Falcon* hover over Cloud City for 20 minutes until a docking bay is available?

Turning this convention on its side was a 1992 *Seinfeld* episode called "The Parking Space." George Costanza (Jason Alexander) gets in an argument with the jerk who nabbed his spot in front of Jerry's apartment building. It drags on for hours. (Of course, had a *CSI* detective needed to park there, the spot would have been open.)

THE IRON THRONE

Q: How does Iron Man go to the bathroom?

A: Even superheroes need to go potty. But taking a break in the middle of an epic battle against the forces of evil isn't always an option. Being the brilliant entrepreneur that he is, Tony "Iron Man" Stark came up with an innovative solution. (Well, for himself at least. His fellow Avengers have to use the nearest bush.) As Stark demonstrated during a scene in 2010's *Iron Man 2*, when nature calls, he goes to the bathroom in his robotic suit.

The film doesn't provide any specifics, but according to *Iron Man Wiki*, a website devoted to the character, Stark's suits contain a sophisticated filtration system that converts his "super pee" into drinkable water. Yum?

LATER SHOWS

Q: Why do late-night talk shows start at 11:35 p.m.?

A: When it comes to the "Big Three" broadcast networks—NBC, ABC, and CBS—there has always been a give-and-take between the network and the local affiliates. The affiliates have always wanted more time for local news, and local NBC stations finally got their wish in 1991: five extra minutes to cover the Gulf War. But *The Tonight Show* host Johnny Carson didn't like it, and he had about as much power as anyone in the TV business in those days. He was worried his ratings would suffer if his show began after 11:30. But Carson was nearing the end of his run, and he didn't want to get in a big battle with network brass, so he agreed to the late start, as long as it never got later than that. Local NBC affiliates were given 35 minutes to deliver the news.

That, in turn, inspired ABC and CBS affiliates to lobby for the same extension. So when David Letterman moved from NBC to CBS in 1993, his show got an 11:35 start time. ABC followed suit and began airing the news program *Nightline* at five minutes past the hour, and *Jimmy Kimmel Live* premiered in 2003 at 12:05, and then ten years later moved to the 11:35 time slot.

BRO-DANCER

Q: What's a male ballerina called?

A: Despite the dance form's long association with French culture, the word *ballerina* comes from Italian, although many other ballet terms are French words. For example, in most ballet companies, any low-level member of the company would be referred to as a *danseuse* or *danseur* (female and male, respectively.) But "ballerina" is traditionally a title of distinction: the company's principal, star female dancer (or *danseuse*, really). The star male dancer, no longer a mere *danseuer*, is also called a "ballerina."

American ballet companies have used the words *ballerina* and *ballerino*, but that practice is declining. These days, both female and male dancers are generally called "ballet dancers." The principal, or star dancer, is no longer called a ballerina but a *prima ballerina* (for a woman). A male ballet star in the U.S. is more likely to be referred to today as a *danseur noble*.

STICKY SITUATION

Q: What does an orchestra conductor actually do? And what's the deal with the baton?

A: Conductors are odd animals, celebrated and vilified at the same time. Case in point—this old joke: Q: What do all great conductors have in common? A: They're all dead. (Our apologies to all you living conductors out there who think you're great.)

At first, orchestras didn't have conductors. Usually, the musicians would be led by the harpsichordist or first violinist. But as orchestras grew and arrangements became more complex, one of the musicians would put down their instrument to conduct the performance with a series of hand movements.

Before the baton was introduced, some conductors used long staffs to keep time. (That's how French conductor Jean-Baptiste Lully met his end—he was keeping time with his staff one night in 1687 when he impaled his foot with it. He fought off the doctors who tried to amputate the infected toe, and later died from gangrene.)

In addition to the dangers posed by staffs, all they really helped conductors do was to keep time, but more subtle instructions were required, such as when to quiet down or when to up the tempo. Conductors started using hand gestures and even facial cues to give instructions, but as orchestras grew larger, it was harder for the musicians in the back to see. That's when the baton came into use. The first ones were rolled-up pieces of sheet music, or a violin bow, but by the 19th century, wooden batons became the norm.

In regard to what conductors actually do, well, it depends on the conductor. Each one develops his or her own style based on the type of music being played and their relationship with the orchestra, choir, big band, etc. It's not too dissimilar from a movie director. Just like actors, the musicians have already learned their parts through hours of rehearsal. They know the notes and the tempos already. What a conductor does is to make sure, during a performance, that they're not veering off from that. Through a series of hand waves, baton waves, facial instructions, and sometimes even what resembles dance moves, they will keep the musicians unified, coordinated, and make sure one section isn't going too fast or slow, or playing too loudly or quietly.

The profession requires someone with a thick skin

and the ability to rein in dozens of disparate personalities and egos, which may explain why conductors get such a bad rap.

CALLING MR. BROWN

Q: Why are there no adults shown in the *Peanuts* comic strips?

A: According to creator Charles Schulz, "There just isn't any room for them. They'd have to bend over to fit in the panels. If you added adults, you'd have to back off and it would change the whole perspective."

MEN IN TIGHTS

Q: Why do most superheroes wear their underwear on the outside?

A: Blame Superman—he started the trend. When he was created in the late 1930s, Superman wore an outfit that was inspired by circus acrobats and professional wrestlers of the day. They weren't necessarily wearing underpants, but tight shorts—shaped like briefs—over the top of their leggings. Because superheroes were super strong—just like wrestlers and acrobats—it wasn't a huge stretch back then for artists to dress them like that. (The most recent on-screen Superman, played by Henry Cavill, is the first one to wear plain blue pants.)

THE ENDING STORY

Q: **Why does a story called *The Neverending Story* have an ending?**

A: *The Neverending Story* is one of the best-known cult films of the 1980s. It featured a timeless story, cool special effects, and unique characters like the flying "luck dragon" Falkor. However, many fans of the film might not know that it's actually based on a novel of the same name that was published in 1979 by German author Michael Ende.

The film covers only about half of the novel and never quite explains why its story is "neverending." Its source material continues to follow the adventures of Bastian and his magical friends over the course of another 200 pages. Instead of saving the kingdom of Fantasia with the power of his own imagination while reading an enchanted book about it (which happens in the film), Bastian becomes confused when the book mysteriously begins repeating its tale over and over again.

Flabbergasted, he eventually realizes that the only way this neverending story will end is if he himself intervenes in the story. After doing so, he's magically transported into Fantasia, where he encounters all of the characters he was reading about. There he begins a new quest while contending with a magical amulet that slowly begins erasing his memories of his life back on Earth. To find out how the novel actually ends, well, we suggest you buy a copy or check it out from your local library.

LANGUAGE

GET A LONG, LITTLE WORD

Q: Why is "abbreviation" such a long word?

A: Even though this word weighs in at five syllables, it began as the much shorter Latin term *brevis*, which means "short." The prefix *ad-* was added, which means "motion to" (later changed to *ab-* because "adbrevis" was hard to say). The suffix *-ated* indicates past tense, making the word mean "something was shortened in the past."

Abbreviations themselves—though in use since ancient times—became widespread after the introduction of the printing press. Every letterform the printer used added time, space, and expense to printed works, so shortcuts were often taken to minimize them. Interestingly, the word "abbreviation" not only held onto its longer form, but today the word can be abbreviated three ways: abbr., abbrv., or abbrev.

ROAD TO NOWHERE

Q: Why do we drive on a parkway but park on a driveway?

A: Don't let the names fool you. A "parkway" doesn't refer to parked vehicles. The term predates cars. If you told someone 150 years ago that you were parking, it would mean that you were planting trees, shrubs, and flowers in a public space. Henceforth, these areas became known as "parks." And the original parkways were roads that went through or connected parks. As the automobile began to overtake the horse-and-buggy, buggy drivers often gathered in these parks to give their horses a break from the loud cars. That's how the verb "park" came to mean "come to a rest." The term "parkway" has remained (in the U.S., anyway) to describe roads that go through wooded areas from park to park.

So what about "driveway"? In the olden days, most big houses (before they were all squeezed together like they are today) were located far from the main road, so people needed a "way" to "drive" their buggies—and later, their cars—to their home. So as the length of driveways shrunk to their present size, the term "drive-way" stuck, even if most modern driveways are only the length of one car.

GOBBLE GOBBLE

Q: **Where did the phrase "talk turkey" come from?**

A: It certainly didn't come from talking turkeys, because turkeys can't talk. The phrase, which means "let's dispense with the small talk and get down to business," goes back to the Pilgrims who settled in Massachusetts in the 17th century. Whenever they traded with the local Indians, no matter what else the Pilgrims wanted, they usually wanted turkeys, too. The request became so commonplace that eventually, the Indians who greeted them would just say, "Let's talk turkey."
Bonus Fact: Benjamin Franklin hated the eagle. He

called it a "bird of bad moral character." He lobbied for the turkey to be America's national bird, but he was overruled.

THE NAME GAME

Q: How is "Peggy" short for "Margaret"?

A: There are a lot of ways to shorten Margaret. For example, there's Greta, Gretchen, Marge, Margie, Maggie, Madge, Maisie, Meg, and most bafflingly, Daisy and Peggy. Daisy comes from the French—*marguerite* is the French word for "daisy," so that one makes sense. Peggy, however, stems from a medieval trend of swapping out letters in names to create rhyming nicknames. It's how Richard can be shortened to Rick and then Dick, and it's also how Margaret becomes Peggy: Margaret becomes Meg, which becomes Peg, and then it's a short leap to Peggy.

Here's another one. The name Henry first became popular in medieval England, although in the Netherlands, the Dutch form, Hendrick, took hold. In Dutch, a nickname for Hendrick is Henk (not Hend), and it was Anglicized to Hank.

Here's one more: John was a common name in England around the time of the Norman conquest in the 11th century. To make the name diminutive, the way we would turn John into Johnny, Normans added "kin," to John, creating "Johnkin." That was shortened over time to Jenkin and then corrupted into Jakin, and ultimately Jack.

A REAL NOWHERE MAN

Q: **Why are unidentified people referred to as "John Doe" and "Jane Doe"?**

A: When the identity of a crime victim or suspect isn't known by police, they still need a way to identify the person for clerical purposes. So police and the media refer to these yet-to-be-named individuals as John Doe or Jane Doe (depending on gender). John Doe was chosen because it's an unremarkable name, and yet also not a common name.

The practice goes all the way back English court-rooms in the 13th century. There was a legal matter called an "action of ejectment," which landlords called upon to quickly and easily eject squatters or delinquent tenants on "behalf" of a fictional third party. That was the person who had issue with the squatter or rent defaulter...but was acting anonymously out of fear of repercussions. That third party didn't exist, of course (it was the landlord trying to act quickly), but they were always identified as "John Doe" or "Jane Doe."

When the English court system was adopted by its colonies in North America, John Doe came along. It's still used in court to protect the anonymity of a witness or victim...unless there are more than one anonymous parties involved in the case. In such an instance, "Roe" is used, as in the famous *Roe v. Wade* trial in the 1970s.

TOTAL RECALL

Q: What did they call a photographic memory before the invention of photography?

A: The technical term for photographic memory is *eidetic memory*, and it existed long before people started taking pictures. "Photographic memory" is really just a layman's term—and an imperfect one at that—to make the phenomenon easier to understand. In this sense, "photographic" refers to a person's ability to recall greatly detailed information very quickly—instantaneously, like how a photo is taken. Sometimes that information comes in images, and a person is considered eidetic if they can remember a great number of details about an image, especially if they only saw it once for a brief time. Eidetic memory can also be used to describe the mental capacity to recall tiny details of sounds or smells after a brief exposure.

Unlike a photograph, eidetic memory doesn't last forever—it's found primarily in children and almost always fades by the age of six, when verbal development has taken over as the brain's main method of communication.

AN IN-TENSE QUESTION

Q: Why do they call it a "building" if it's already been built?

A: Like similar words including "drive" and "walk," "building" is both a noun and a verb. It can refer to the process of constructing a building or the end product itself. Its roots go all the way back to *timbran*, an Old English word once used to describe the act of building wooden structures.

After the Normans arrived in England in 1066, Old English gradually evolved into a new version that we call Middle English. Flash forward to the 13th century when English people started using *byldan* instead. It came from *buthlam*, a Proto-Germanic word. *Timbran* was eventually forgotten while *byldan* eventually evolved into "build" and "building" (the latter of which was only used to describe structures) sometime in the 15th century. In the years that followed, people started mixing up the two words, so "building" can now mean both "a building" and "the process of building a building."

PULP NONFICTION

Q: Which came first, the color orange, or the fruit that bears its name?

A: The citrus fruit was discovered long before the word "orange" entered the English language. Around the year A.D. 800, traders from the Arabian Peninsula by way of Southeast Asia brought oranges to Spain. They called the round, sweet fruit *naranj*, derived from *naranga*, a Sanskrit word that referred to an orange tree.

Over the next few centuries, the fruit's popularity spread to England, and by the 1300s, the name became Anglicized. *Naranj* became *naranja*, then *norange*, and finally "orange." The word "orange," as in the color, wasn't used until the early 1540s. Between the 1300s and 1600s, English speakers (and printers) just didn't think to use the exotic fruit's shade to refer to something that was the same color. Instead they used words like "reddish," "amber," or "tawny."

Bonus Fact: Have you heard the adage that nothing rhymes with orange? It's not true. Well, *almost* nothing rhymes with orange. The only English or English-adjacent words that rhyme with orange are:

1) Blorenge, the name of a mountain in Wales.

2) Sporange, a sac in some plants where spores are reproduced and stored.

NUTTY AS A FRUITCAKE

Q: Why do "nuts" and "bananas" mean "crazy"?

A: Not until the 19th century did the Western world begin to view mental illness as a serious public health issue. Back then, most mentally ill people were feared, ridiculed, or believed to be possessed by the devil. They were often homeless or institutionalized. And the words used to describe them were often demeaning.

Plenty of lighthearted synonyms came about to connote "crazy," or more specifically, "weird," or "not quite right." Two of the most inexplicable have stood the test of time: "nuts" and "bananas."

In the 1850s, calling one's head a "nut" was a popular slang expression. That makes sense, because your head is fairly nutlike—it's round and the important stuff (your brain) is protected by a thick shell (your skull). By the 1860s, the expression "off one's nut," meant "weird," "crazy," etc. By the 1930s, the expression had been truncated to "nuts." (In the UK, it had morphed into "nutter.")

The usage of "bananas" as a stand-in for "crazy" comes from several corruptions and adaptations of the slang use of the word "bent." In the 1910s, "bent" was used by criminals to describe other criminals they thought were crooked (meaning working with the police). By the 1930s, "bent" meant "illegal," but it also came to mean that someone was "a bit off." Before long, the word "bananas" took the place of "bent," because bananas are bent.

MEAN MEAT

Q: Why is it meat jerky called "jerky"?

A: The English word for dried or cured meat comes from the Quechua language, spoken in the Andes region of South America since before the time of the Incas. Their word *ch'arki* means "dried flesh." Spanish explorers, possibly as early as the 1500s, borrowed it and it became the Spanish word *charqui*. That migrated to English, and by the 1840s it had become "jerky."

The word "jerk," as in "that guy's a real jerk," has a different history, but it's unclear how it got started. One possibility is that it's carnival slang from the 1930s to describe undesirable people from "jerkwater towns."

That term, "jerkwater," comes from tiny railroad towns where steam engines would be filled with water by "jerking," or pulling really hard, on a lever to drop the water into the train. That term is medieval, and it comes from the sound a whip makes—"jerk!"—when it's used to strike a horse. (And while we're at it, that led to the term "soda jerk" to describe a young store clerk in the 1940s who would pour sodas and make floats for customers by "jerking" a lever.)

STOOPID DICKTIONARY!

Q: What happens when a dictionary spells a word incorrectly?

A: Dictionaries don't spell words incorrectly because dictionary makers exhaustively research the words before they add them to the latest edition. For example, the *Oxford English Dictionary* is staffed with the world's most authoritative experts in the fields of linguistics and literature. One of their tasks is to add new words to the dictionary, so that it can be a living, changing canon of the English language. But before they do, staffers thoroughly research prospective words to gauge how common and pervasive they are in media, in daily conversations, and in literature. If a word has been vetted and is deemed viable, it's short-listed for inclusion in the next edition of the dictionary. At that point, a spelling is chosen. If the word is spelled multiple ways, dictionary publishers research the word some more to determine its most common spelling.

GO FIGYER

Q: Why isn't "phonetic" spelled "funettik"?

A: Most of the words and phrases we use today are hundreds or even thousands of years old. They've had long histories and etymologies, developed over a long time, and descended from several different languages. Take the word "phonetic," which refers to the science of sounds and the study of word pronunciation. It comes from the Greek word *phonetikos*, meaning "vocal." Like most—if not all—other words in the English language connoting an academic discipline, "phonetic" is Greek, so it's spelled in an Anglicized version of the Greek root word. If it were derived from an English word from the beginning, it would probably be spelled a lot closer to the way it sounds.

HAPPY EVER EITHER

Q: Is "either" pronounced "ee-ther" or "ay-ther"?

A: "Eee-thur" is the preferred way. (And so is "nee-thur.")

LET DOWN YOUR GARD

Q: Is or isn't "irregardless" a word?

A: When you type "irregardless" into a text message or a Word document, the squiggly red line appears underneath it to inform you that it is misspelled. Take away the "ir" at the beginning, and you're left with "regardless," which has no squiggly red line. So that makes it official—"irregardless" is not a word. Right? Not quite.

According to Merriam-Webster, which has an entry for the non-word that people love to hate, "The most frequently repeated remark about 'irregardless' is that 'there is no such word.' There is such a word, however." It has been used (mistakenly) in place of "regardless" since the early 1900s and has now been admitted into dictionaries. So even though it technically is a word, "irregardless" is still far from being widely accepted. And judging by the scorn it receives online, it won't be widely accepted anytime soon. Merriam-Webster's advice: "Use regardless instead."

SOME QUESTIONS HAVE NO ANSWERS

"If bankers can count, how come they have ten windows and two tellers?"

—MILTON BERLE

THE HUMAN
CONDITION

INTO THIN AIR

Q: Why does inhaling helium make your voice high?

A: Speech is comprised of sound waves that are created when air moves past your vocal cords, which stretch horizontally across the larynx. The air makes those cords vibrate, moving air molecules around at different frequencies to create the various sounds that make up speech. (Other factors are involved, too, such as how you move your tongue and your lips.)

One of the main factors that affects speech is the quality of the air. Regular air is more than 80 percent nitrogen (and one-fifth oxygen). Nitrogen has a heavy molecular mass relative to helium. In fact, helium is so light that it's literally lighter than the air (which, again, is mostly nitrogen). Because it's so light, sound waves travel quicker through helium that they do through nitrogen-based air—about three times as fast. Inhaling helium changes the air molecules moving across your vocal cords, and ultimately makes your voice move faster. To the ear, this sounds higher.

A MAMMARY MYSTERY

Q: Why do men have nipples?

A: A human's gender is determined by the chromosomes contained within the sperm that fertilizes the mother's egg. Everyone begins life in utero as female, but if the sperm contains a Y chromosome, they'll start becoming male at around the two-month mark of fetal development. Nipples start forming before that point and continue to grow throughout the remainder of the pregnancy. So even though males don't develop the rest of the of components that would have made them female, the nipples remain.

SOME QUESTIONS HAVE NO ANSWERS

"What are perfect strangers? Do they have perfect hair? Do they dress perfectly?"

—ELLEN DEGENERES

HAIR-RAISING QUESTION

Q: Why can men grow facial hair but women can't?

A: First off, women can and do grow facial hair, just not nearly as much as men do. This is due to *androgens*, a compound that controls the development and maintenance of male characteristics such as growing thick facial hair. The best known androgen: testosterone. Both males and females have androgens coursing through their bodies, but men have a lot more of them.

For the average woman, androgens only cause hair to grow on their legs, private parts, and under their armpits. There are some women, however, who have enough androgen to grow facial hair or even wind up with a hairy chest.

STINKY SYMPHONY

Q: Why do beans make people fart?

A: We've all sung the famous song:

> *Beans, beans, the musical fruit,*
> *the more you eat, the more you toot,*
> *the more you toot, the better you feel,*
> *so let's have beans for every meal!*

The main reason beans cause you to fart: the small intestine, where food is broken down into microscopic bits so the nutritious parts can be absorbed, can't entirely process beans.

Beans contain *oligosaccharides*, a group of sugars that can't easily be absorbed into the walls of your guts. Instead, they're sent on a roller-coaster ride to your bowels, where they'll encounter hundreds of different types of bacteria that feast on the oligosaccharides. When the bacteria's meal is finished, they emit gases such as methane and hydrogen. All those gases begin to build up and start forming flatulence.

If you're eager to torture your friends, dried navy and lima beans tend to cause the most gas. Canned beans, which lose a lot of their oligosaccharides during the production process, don't create as much. If you'd prefer to avoid flatulence, drain the water out of each can before you cook the beans.

MOVING RIGHT ALONG

Q: Why do prunes, uh, work so well?

A: In recent years, fruit packagers have tried to "rebrand" prunes as "dried plums," so as to downplay the one thing that everybody knows (and appreciates, on occasion) about prunes: they help make bowel movements when bowel movements just aren't happening on their own.

The dietary element most associated with good bowel movements is fiber, found in moderate to large quantities in most fruits, vegetables, grains, and legumes. Plums, as well as prunes, are rich in fiber. But that's not what helps relieve constipation. Helping the fiber do its job is *diphenyl isatin*, a naturally occurring laxative abundant in prunes. Also, a single prune contains more than a gram each of *sorbitol*. Used as a low-calorie sugar substitute, sorbitol is pretty much impossible for the human body to digest. Result: it literally goes right through you...and it takes whatever was sitting in your stomach and colon along for the ride.

REALLY QUITE MAD

Q: Will contracting rabies really make you go insane?

A: An untreated case of rabies can lead to some very unpleasant health problems followed by, in most cases, death. This infectious disease is typically spread via the bites of infected animals—most commonly dogs, bats, and raccoons. Symptoms can take anywhere from a week to even a year to start showing. They often begin with a fever followed by a headache and weird, tingling sensations near where the victim was bit.

Without immediate medical attention, the disease will progress in one of two different ways. An estimated 30 percent of untreated human cases result in *paralytic rabies*. The victim succumbs to paralysis before falling into a coma and dying.

The other, more common type, called *furious rabies*, really does make you go mad. First comes hyperactivity, followed by paranoia, insomnia, hallucinations, and the sudden onset of intense fears, most often of water. Your body produces large amounts of saliva, which causes foaming at the mouth. After another day or two, you'll succumb to cardiorespiratory arrest and die.

Fortunately, the disease can be cured if you seek medical attention within 10 days. But once the symptoms start appearing, survival becomes increasingly unlikely. The development of vaccinations for dogs and other household pets has helped reduce the average number of annual human deaths in the United States to under two.

CRAZY TALK

Q: What's the difference between a sociopath and a psychopath?

A: "Sociopath" and "psychopath" are often used interchangeably to describe people who commit heinous crimes (if they're not just called "insane" by lawyers, doctors, and the media, that is). But they are two very different "antisocial personality disorders" that exhibit similar symptoms, as well as some that overlap.

Among the commonalities, both sociopaths and psychopaths have a disregard for the law and moral codes, they don't feel remorse, and they have violent tendencies.

Here's where they differ. Sociopaths generally exhibit nervous personalities, including emotional outbursts and moments of rage. They have a hard time forming relationships, generally live alone, and have difficulty in laying down roots and holding jobs. Violent crimes committed by sociopaths are much more likely to be spontaneous, the result of a moment of uncontrolled rage or an emotional outburst.

Psychopaths, on the other hand, cannot form real emotional attachments to others, although they learn to imitate empathy (and other inviting emotions) so as to win the trust of others with whom they can create superficial relationships. Always calm and collected, a psychopath's violent crimes are carefully planned out ahead of time.

The causes are also different, and it comes down to "nature vs. nurture." Psychiatric studies suggest that sociopathy is the result of poor brain development brought on by environmental causes (such as an extremely troubled childhood). Psychopathy is a genetic abnormality or early development issue.

GESUNDHEIT!

Q: **If you kept your eyes open when you sneezed, would they pop out?**

A: Sneezes cause you to exert quite a bit of energy, but not enough for your eyes to pop out of their sockets. The reason you close your eyes when you sneeze: it's an involuntary reflex. The nerves that go to both your eyes and nose are closely connected, so when something happens to one of them, it can affect the other. (This is why some people sneeze when they see bright light.)

OUT, OUT DAMN TOXIN!

Q: **Do you really "sweat out toxins" when you exercise?**

A: If only that were true. Sweat's one and only duty is to cool off the body. As such, it's made up of water and trace minerals. Toxins are processed through the liver and kidneys, and then excreted when you go to the bathroom.

> ## SOME QUESTIONS
> ## HAVE NO ANSWERS
>
> "Why do they call it rush hour when nothing moves?"
>
> **—ROBIN WILLIAMS (AS MORK)**

ONLY SKIN DEEP

Q: **If skin is always renewing itself, why don't scars completely heal, and why don't tattoos disappear?**

A: If scars and tattoos were located on the surface your skin, they would only last about 28 days. That's how long it takes for your *epidermis*, the outer layer of skin, to renew itself. New cells push up the old cells, which die off and then float around your house and settle on your furniture. But the type of trauma that leads to scars and tattoos goes deeper, down into the *dermis*. The cells in scar tissue don't die off, so the scar remains.

Similarly, the ink in tattoos is injected all the way into the dermis, which is why getting a tattoo hurts so much (unless you're really drunk).

So if tattoos never go away, why do they fade? A few reasons: first, if the ink wasn't injected deep enough into the dermis, it will gradually fade as the epidermis replaces itself over and over. Also, if you didn't provide proper care for your tattoo right after you got it, some of the ink may escape the skin. That's why you should keep new ink as dry as possible.

GOING VIRAL

Q: **What is the common cold, and why is there no cure for it?**

A: A virus is nothing but a very small piece of DNA that makes copies of itself. Wrap the DNA snippet in a protective shell made of protein material, and you've got a virus. Because viruses are so small, scientists couldn't really isolate and identify them until the invention of the electron microscope in the 1930s. Naturally, the first viruses that people studied were the ones that made them sick. Humans suffer from a long list of viral illnesses—including smallpox, AIDS, influenza, hepatitis, and even some types of cancer. The common cold is also viral and serves as a good case study to explain the basic life cycle of all viruses.

The virus that causes colds is known as *human rhinovirus* (HRV), and its only purpose is to reproduce itself. It does this by invading the cells that make up the surface of your nose, throat, and lungs. Once inside a cell, HRV acts like a computer hacker, plugging scraps of foreign DNA into the cell's genetic material and reprogramming it—basically ordering it to reproduce itself and, thereby, produce new copies of the virus. The host cell soon fills with so many new copies of HRV that it bursts and dies.

All the classic symptoms of a cold—stuffy nose, sore throat, cough, and fever—aren't actually caused by the virus. Those are the by-product of the human immune system fighting off the viral attack. Fortunately, your immune system is strong enough to eventually kill off the invaders, but by that time, the HRV has probably moved on, using the runny nose and cough the body produces to spread to another person.

So the reason there's "no cure for the common cold" is that the cold itself is the cure. It just takes a while.

BE QUIET SO MY EARS CAN SEE!

Q: **Why do we turn down the music in the car when we're trying to find our destination?**

A: It's all about your mind's ability—or lack thereof—to multitask. Different regions of the brain perform different tasks. That's called "attentional capacity," and there's only so much to go around. So when the radio is blaring and your passengers are yapping, your brain, while trying to pay attention to the road, is also busy processing all of that auditory information. And that doesn't stop when you suddenly realize that you can't find the street address you're looking for. Now that you're lost, you need your visual center to work extra hard to find your destination. To do that, your brain has to stop processing auditory information. Solution: turn down the radio and tell your passengers to zip it. It's for this very reason that fighter pilots wear noise-canceling headphones.

SIMPLE MINDS

Q: **Do we really use only 10 percent of our brains?**

A: What good would a brain be if nearly all of it remained dormant? Not much good at all. We actually use *every* part of our brain, because each section performs a different function—from creating abstract thoughts, to processing external stimuli, to keeping you balanced. But your brain is also good at saving energy, so it only activates a section when it is needed. That's why brain scans often show that most of the brain is quiet, because at any given time, only about 10 percent of your brain cells are active.

It's unclear where this myth comes from (some have wrongly attributed it to Albert Einstein), but it predates the technology required to perform brain scans. For example, in the forward of the 1936 book *How to Win Friends and Influence People* by Dale Carnegie, Lowell Thomas wrote: "Professor William James of Harvard used to say that the average man develops only ten percent of his latent mental ability."

In the 1970s, the New Age movement took hold of this idea to put forth that most of humankind's true abilities have yet to be tapped because so much of our brains remain dormant; if we could "turn them on," then we could master telekinesis, ESP, and other supernatural abilities. Sadly, it's not true.

PERCHANCE TO DREAM

Q: **Why do we have to sleep?**

A: On the surface, it seems like a great blunder of evolution—to require a living thing to fall into an unconscious, paralyzed, defenseless state for several hours every single day.

So what gives? The function of sleep is still not completely understood by scientists. One thing is certain: all creatures great and small have to endure a period of rest every day, including mammals, fish, birds, reptiles, and insects—basically, anything with a central nervous system. And many flora and microbes (which lack a central nervous system) also exhibit *circadian rhythms*, a 24-hour biological cycle that responds primarily to light and darkness in the environment. (But that doesn't necessarily mean that plants sleep.)

With humans, it works like this: our circadian cycle kicks in when sunlight enters our eyes in the morning. Brain cells that control *melatonin* levels (a hormone that anticipates the daily onset of darkness) are turned on. When the day ends, melatonin production increases, making you drowsy. Then you sleep until morning, and start the cycle over again. This *diurnal* behavior goes back to the time when our ancestors lived in caves. Retreating into safe shelters every night not only kept early humans safe, but it gave their brains and bodies an opportunity to rest and recharge, and for injuries to heal.

To find out why our bodies need sleep, researchers look at what happens when we go without it. Sleep-deprivation experiments have revealed that people who are denied a good night's rest have more trouble doing, well, everything. Their memory is compromised, they're more irritable, and their health begins to suffer. Go without sleep for long enough, and you'll suffer from hallucinations and, in rare cases, death.

In one experiment, researchers placed several rats into a maze, and they had to figure out how to navigate it (the rats, not the researchers). Then the rats were put to bed. That night, the researchers let half of the rats have an undisturbed night of sleep; the other group had their sleep interrupted several times. The next morning, the sleep-deprived rats performed even worse inside the maze than the night before. And the other group not only navigated the maze successfully, but some actually did it faster than the previous night. So that means that sleep, in addition to helping retain memory, also helps you hone new skills. (In fact, if you're a student and you have a big test in the morning, don't stay up all night cramming. Instead, review your notes once and then get a good night's sleep so your brain will be a better test-taker.)

WORKING OVERTIME

Q: What's going on in our brains while we sleep?

A: A whole lot. Being the advanced computer that it is, your brain spends much of the evening "defragging" all the information your senses experienced during your waking hours, when it was working nonstop to first decipher those inputs and then integrate them by building new neural connections. But your head computer has limits, so most of that input gets stored away until you sleep. Then it's time to sort through all the data and clear out all the waste your brain doesn't need (by breaking connections) and to solidify the information it wants to retain (by strengthening connections).

And there's another aspect of sleep that plays into this: dreaming.

PERCHANCE TO LEARN

Q: Why do we dream?

A: If you're an average adult, you spend at least one hour every night in a state of REM (rapid eye movement) sleep—that's when most dreaming occurs. REM is exactly what it sounds like: your eyes are literally looking around at things created by your imagination. As far as *why* dreaming occurs, scientists are still trying to pinpoint the exact reason. One thing is known: all mammals dream, as do birds.

For humans, dreaming is a huge part or our lives. When you were a baby, you spent up to 50 percent of your sleep time dreaming. That gives credence to the prevailing theory that dreams help us learn things. In one study, adults who were taking a language course dreamed more each night than a second group who weren't taking a class.

So dreams, it seems, give your brain a chance to perform functions it couldn't do during the day. Much like the purpose of sleep (see the previous question), dreams may help us decipher the events of the day and figure out what's important to retain (how to conjugate Latin verbs), and what doesn't need to stick around (the teacher's boring stories). So if dreams are so instrumental in helping us out, why…that sounds like a separate question.

IT SEEMED SURREAL!

Q: Why are dreams so weird?

A: Let's say, for instance, that you're worried about losing your job, so you have a dream where you're in the middle of the desert looking in vain for your key card to get into the building where you work. If you're worried about losing your job, why not just dream about actually *losing your job*?

Sometimes you do. Dreams are separated into two basic categories, literal and symbolic. It's the symbolism that's so confusing. There are a plethora of theories as to what dreams mean, and it's all but impossible to find a consensus.

In a 2006 *Scientific American* article, Ernest Hartmann, the director of the Sleep Disorders Center at Newton Wellesley Hospital in Boston, Massachusetts, wrote that many scientists think of dreams as "simply an epiphenomenon that is the mental activity that occurs during REM sleep." In other words, dreams are nothing more than a by-product of a busy brain producing random images that don't really mean anything. But Hartmann and many of his colleagues don't hold to this way of thinking; they posit that all that weird symbolism is trying to tell you something. They call this the "Contemporary Theory of Dreaming," which Hartmann describes thusly:

> Activation patterns are shifting and connections are being made and unmade constantly in our brains, forming the physical basis for our minds.

At one end of the continuum is focused waking activity, such as when we are doing an arithmetic problem. Here our mental functioning is focused, linear and well-bounded. When we move from focused waking to looser waking thought—reverie, daydreaming, and finally dreaming—mental activity becomes less focused, looser, more global and more imagistic. Dreaming is the far end of this continuum: the state in which we make connections most loosely.

During this less-focused state of being, Hartmann says the images are not random, but that they are "instead guided by the emotions of the dreamer." So (unless you practice lucid dreaming) you may not be able to control your dreams, but your emotions are controlling them for you.

For example, someone who has recently suffered a terrible trauma—like a fire—will dream more frequently, and the dreams will be more intense. But the dreams may not necessarily be about fire. Instead, one might be a nightmare about outrunning angry people dressed in red shirts. The imagery may not match the event that triggered the dream, but the emotion is the same—in this case, terror. As time passes, the intensity of the dreams will gradually become milder, but the emotion may stay present in other dreams for some time.

"When the emotional state is less clear," Hartmann continues, "the dream becomes more complicated. The dream appears to be somehow 'connecting up' or 'weaving in' the new material in the mind, which suggests a possible function." And function, though difficult to prove, is what dreaming may be all about. "In the immediate sense, making these connections and tying things down diminishes the emotional disturbance or arousal. In the longer term, the traumatic material is connected with other parts of the memory systems so that it is no longer so unique or extreme—the idea being that the next time something similar or vaguely similar occurs, the connections will already be present and the event will not be quite so traumatic."

This was important for our ancestors, because they dealt with a lot more trauma—from rivals, predators, and harsh environmental conditions—than we do today. So the function of dreaming for early humans was to "weave this new material into the memory system." If this theory is true (which Hartmann is quick to note it hasn't been proven), then the answer to our question is that we dream about weird things so they can be tied into our lives on an emotional level. Or, as lucid dreamer and *Huffpost* blogger Dr. Angel Morgan put it, "Dreams help us know ourselves better."

THE END

Q: **Why do we die?**

A: If only we were graced with *negligible senescence*, we might be able to live forever. Senescence, the scientific term for "growing old," afflicts most, but not all, creatures on Earth. The cells of tortoises and lobsters, for example, don't degrade over time like ours do. So unless these animals become sick or gravely injured,

they could conceivably live forever. But these animals are a tiny minority in a world full of species that experience cellular degradation, which leads to weaker systems, and ultimately death. In fact, some animals, like the mayfly, live for less than a day. Why?

Theologians and philosophers have been debating this for millennia. According to the Bible, we don't really die, we just leave our mortal coil at some point: "The dust returns to the ground it came from, and the spirit returns to God who gave it." (Ecclesiastes 12:7, NIV).

In scientific terms, the biological predisposition to death is tied directly to natural selection and evolution. In 2015, the website *Phys.org* reported on a game-changing study conducted by scientists at the New England Complex Systems Institute, and the Wyss Institute for Biologically Inspired Engineering at Harvard University. Their conclusion: we're genetically programmed to die.

That goes against the long-held notion of natural selection that "only the strong survive." How could a gradual demise caused by cellular degradation help a species thrive? Because evolution does not favor the individual but the group as a whole. One of the study's lead scientists, Dr. Justin Werfel, explains it like this:

> It seems intuitively obvious that a gene contributing to the death of its owner ought to be selected against. That idea is consistent with standard theories, which conclude that it's impossible for selection to act in favor of shortened lifespan directly—the only way a lifespan-shortening gene could be favored is if it also increases reproduc-

tion earlier in life, so that it gives a net benefit to the individual. However, what we see in spatial models is that longer-lived variants deplete their environment more, and as a result wind up with fewer chances to reproduce, so that self-limited lifespan actually winds up giving an advantage far enough down the line.

To reiterate, the reason you have to die one day is so that future generations can survive. It may be the last selfless act you ever do.

SOME QUESTIONS HAVE NO ANSWERS

"If ignorance is bliss, why aren't there more happy people in the world?"

—STEPHEN FRY